THE INTENSIT
HUMAN FEELINGS
Born and die, die and born

INMACULADA RODRÍGUEZ

SMART BOOK

Copyright © 2023
Smart Book
The Intensity of the Human Feelings
Born and die, die and born
Written and illustrated by:
Inmaculada Rodriguez

Instagram-Alma Style

Fan page-Alma Rodríguez

WHEN YOU BUY THE PHYSICAL VERSION OF THE OF THE BOOK. GO TO MY FAN AND WRITE AN HONEST REVIEW, AND YOU WILL BE ENTERED AUTOMATICLY INTO A SWEEPSTAKES. PLEASE LEVAE YOUR EMAIL SO WE CAN IDENTIFY YOU.

Table of Contents

Preface

This literacy work, shares experiences lived in different stages of a person, shows the pain, but also teaches us how to get out of depression, stress, and anxiety.

It takes us by the hand in such a way that it is easy to feel involved, because it talks about the experiences in a family relationship, of friends and even in dating, in a very clear and precise way, when it is good to keep fighting for a love and when to stop doing it. It teaches the healthy limits of good friendship, focusing attention on the things we should share and the things we should reserve only for ourselves.

Explicitly, it tells us how the experience is of being deprived of freedom and the timely advice not to do the wrong thing, because it is an experience that can cause madness in people and relates the fear of facing society when finally getting freedom.

It also refers to the inconveniences of romantic love, all the steps you must go through, how much you must wait and above all how much you must give.

This book talks about the consequences of our actions, if we do good, we will receive good, otherwise, we will get drawbacks. This book tells many interesting stories and communicates powerful truths that can inspire and transform mindsets and the intensity of human feelings.

Introduction

All these themes are based on real and lived facts, with the purpose that each one of us identify with these subjects and put them into practice for our divine betterment and to fulfill all the purposes and teachings, which will be useful for the first, second and other generations. In this way to live the earthly life, as we really deserve it and above all to feel human.

The true purpose of this book is to give life to abandoned children, single and pregnant women, and to care for the elderly. But most importantly, is to help people who have terminal illnesses and tragic accidents, with the title Los Angeles del Cielo, together we can be one, in addition, we must understand that feeling of peace that makes us live as the noblest human beings, as our God wants, this emotion must come from our heart, because otherwise, the joy will not be equal, without forgetting that the most beautiful thing is to feel it and live it.

I was inspired for all these topics by my Lord Jesus Christ, who has never forsaken me. He is the only one who truly motivated me to write all these wonders, who teaches us the difficulties and much learning during our lives, the beauty of it all, is that we never finish learning.

I also want to thank a great person who always believed in me, his name is Keith Logan; since he always pushed me to do what he believed would be an example for all of us.

Biography

Ever since I was a little girl, I always had it in my mind to succeed in life. I remember wondering what I wanted to do when I grew up. I dreamed of being an actress, but life had other plans for me. I couldn't be an actress, and at that time I discovered an unconditional love for humanity.

As I became a woman, I always kept that in my mind, even if people hurt me, I tried to analyze why they did it or if they acted out of ignorance, it helped me to forget their actions. Rather, I was looking for a way to make them change or be a little more flexible.

There was a moment when I started to think about whether it was a temporary thing that was happening to me. It happened several times, when I had another human being, get hurt by me, obviously, they were going to react like all of them did. I was always looking for the positive side of any negative situation. Even though my life has been one of too much suffering, I didn't like to see another person suffer because I already knew beforehand what it felt like.

I realized that in any other situation I wanted to see what those people were going through, so I could bring them some happiness. During my difficult life something happened where I didn't know how I was going to react, and that was when I was separated from my family who are my motivation and my joy.

That's when I knew what my positive reactions were going to be against life and the people around me, and whether I was going to remain who I always was or become a person without feelings. It seemed unnatural; my sufferings were innumerable. I could not spend all my time thinking about them and not caring about the sufferings of others. But it was just the opposite. Instead of thinking about all my problems I realized that I liked helping others, it was uncontrollable. I always thought of helping others to smile, although, in my mind I had ideals and dreams, which sometimes are not so easy to fulfill. Finally, with the help of God my Lord, I decided to write this book, in my mind I am sure that I will be able to fulfill my dream of seeing smiles in all the people that don't have him, so we could smile together.

That's why I decided to call this book, Human Feelings: because everyone has feelings, we just sometimes don't know if they are alive or dead. If only we all thought about how the hearts of the abandoned children, the elderly without families and those who have nothing to eat feel.
The dreams that due to lack of support end up on the street, in gangs or dead (just ask alma).
People without a home who have nowhere to live, pregnant women who decide to abort because they have no economic support. These are my daily thoughts, without stopping, at the same time, to see those dreams of helping each other, come true.

The purpose of this book is based on the collection of funds from every country, for the Angels of Heaven project, which is already designed and thought out, where each one of the neediest would be helped.

This theme has a lot to do with the angels of heaven, since it will be the starting point for the solution of all our needs; we, as human beings, will be the angels of heaven by putting a grain of sand to cover human needs.

Initial design by **Inmaculada Rodrígue**z. Your dream comes true. The **Villa Angel Sky** ecotourism project is a project with the highest standards of quality and comfort. **Angel Sky** has its initial idea inspired by the owner of the project (**Inmaculada Rodriguez**).

Villa Angel Sky, the architect inspired by the architecture of ancient Rome with an essential touch of modern architecture, the rooms have a 360-degree panoramic view, within the common areas, we have the living room, an open concept space with dining room, kitchen, bar, TV room and pool. Already on the second level, up an elegant staircase, we are released to an outdoor space full of beautiful nature and an event room decorated with metal profiles that gives a unique touch to the project. Finally, in the private area, we have 5 independent rooms in the highest part of the project.

Wisdom prayer

Many of us human beings for some reason or another face different adversities in our daily lives. We immigrate to the United States and face racism; we live with worry, criticism and do not respect what country or language we come from.

We get confused, which leads us to make mistakes. We live passionately and have patience, surrounded by impatient human beings, we also relate to many without thinking about the storm. We want to be calm, and we sow seeds without reaping fruits.

We all have different religions with very little faith, we give many explanations without understanding the content. We move from one place to another, escaping from problems because we do not have discipline. We live surrounded by danger, causing detentions. We have so much ambition with incomparable challenges, that we even lose our companions. We get involved and focus on sexuality, giving ourselves despite much coldness, our heart only lives in fear and sadness.

We want a new life to achieve a transformation and we only live in illusion, and when we face a divorce for lack of understanding, sometimes we give ourselves with everything and many do not care about our pain. We move from the country to the city looking for healing and we sink into jobs where many of us come to an end because of ambition.

We refuse help because we live in fear and have no consideration. Some of us have so much instability that it leads us to lose respect for humanity. We seek to get answers, but we prefer to be blind and then start over.

Win or lose, we will never understand that.

We want happiness at the risk of our freedom. We abuse the colored, accusing them of being small.

We all want to be reasonable in trusting and giving, but in many cases over time it becomes a fatality.

Many of us think we are so sexy that we become horny, living on emotions and disappointments because loving and wanting is no longer in our plan, and we all live disillusioned, and it seems that our effort was all in vain. We want tranquility and we decide to separate, there comes the teasing if you are fat or skinny then comes the stage of crying.

We trust our friends with sad feelings, without understanding that many are just in the moment!

Encountered planets

Saturn vs Venus

Saturn: You just live from work to bed, and I don't care if anyone complains.

Some may be lucky and perhaps, I can say good night to them. I will try to make a lot of noise, I need to sleep, tomorrow I have a meeting with Jupiter in the office.

Venus: That doesn't surprise me at all, go to sleep, I'm used to it.

Saturn: For a long time I have lived sure of myself, now I feel lonely, I realized that my life has been stolen from me.

Venus: Don't come near me, I wanted to let you know about the nearest earthquake and you didn't care about what was around you. Which was slowly destroying what was already bad. You let yourself go because you were married, you just lived snoring, then you wanted to wake up, but everything was already very clear, now I don't feel abandoned, I know you are very strong with all your people. Maybe later you will understand that if "you snooze you lose".

Saturn: You are right, but I still have the illusion that you love me, I want to fight this tremendous war with you.

Venus: Unfortunately it's too late, I made my decision, I couldn't take it anymore with so many disappointments, because even if I tried, it was worthless, that's why I took all my things and got the hell out, and although it took a lot of, I knew that I had no future by your side.

Saturn: What are you talking about? You belong to me; you must understand that I have the power to make you believe again that everything I have I will share with you and if you want, I can even help your friends.

Venus: I am sorry for you, I already moved on, but right now I wish you luck, if you want you can sue me, I am my own lawyer, I hope you will find somebody that will put up with all the sleepless nights, the same way as I waited for you to turn and look at me, I loved you, that's the reason why I kept waiting through calamity and everything else, I realized that there was no electricity, my body couldn't wait any longer.

Saturn: I always meant to be a gentleman by allowing myself to be carried along, by your love that was very sincere. Now I understand that it was never real, I feel that I am fighting with fire, and I feel that I must become water and extinguish all that ground.

Venus: You are right, but make no mistake, because everything that happened was not temporary, that daily routine, I got tired of sleeping in that cold bed, now I have someone who gives me drinks at night and during the day, so much that he makes me snore... in the middle of the night, he makes me sweat.

Saturn: I just want to know if you are serious, I can't believe it. Nor do I want to understand and see you with someone else, savoring all that love that I didn't know how to give you. If I see you with someone else, I'll forget that I am Saturn and I will come to finish off, that one that you call, "the man who only wants your body."

Venus: Get away from me, you are no longer part of me, now I want to be happy. It was all your fault. I got tired of sleeping in that cold bed, this is all on me, the one I have now, makes me lose focus.

Saturn: I can understand that. I just want to know if in the future we can work together, I like your energy. I already knew that without you my life would die.

Venus: Despite everything, at the end of the day, we are all one, you will survive this storm, you will see, with the passing of time, each one will have their own. I hope you can understand that we, the feminine ones, are not just around the corner.

Death is not eternal.

Alma: _ "Hello, brother, I'm glad you came to see me." _

Jesus: _ "Hello, little sister. Of course, I saw you being born." _

Alma: _"And I saw you with my Sister Miledys, dancing, also when you said with your manly voice, my God, my God, I want to work harder to give my family a better future. But the hardest blow was when I was 9 years old, when I received the news that I would no longer be able to see that brown skin, which only reflected many good things. Now I understand that death is not eternal, because true love makes us see each other in heaven. I want to tell you that I will always fight for you, to be able to see that smile on your brown skin. I want you to know that you live in me, you make me happy.

I have never forgotten you, you are in my shadow, letting me know that you are by my side, I can feel that, after I lost you. I know you left, but you never lost me, you are by my side making sure I made it and that even though you are not here with me, I want to share my continues joy.

I send my love to our departed ones; I hope they are enjoying all the good things. Tell my dad not to worry about anything, because all his children are no longer fighting. I want you to give lots of kisses to our grandparents, they already know that we are enjoying all their fruit together.

Goodbye, little brother, everyone sends you greetings and remember that you are part of my future.

I love you forever.

Inmaculada Rodriguez. _"

Jesus Rodriguez

Love does not come so easy

Since we are children, we are taught that love is the most important thing, just because we are small and innocent children. It causes everyone around us to not want to give affection and we grow up with that need, to receive and give love. In truth it is a need just like wanting to go to the bathroom and get rid of everything that the body rejects, but love does not want to be stripped and it does not matter if someone else receives it.

We made the comparison that it is like stripping everything that the body does not want, but we also know that to strip the body must eat and drink. So, when it comes to loving and wanting it is a little bit similar since, even if it is our father, mother, or brother, I mean the closest ones in our lives. If your father was not with you when you were a child watching you grow up in your difficult stages, as a son or daughter you will not love him as such, and love will not be the same as if you had grown up with him. Just as with the mother, love is the most special thing, and it is kept deep in your heart. It is difficult for you to bring it to the surface and show it properly.

When you are siblings, even if you are blood and not raised together, love is not going to do the same. So, we see if love comes or originates just because it has your blood. But no, love reproduces itself day by day. It is as if you go to a job that every day you must go, with the difference that love is more sensitive, that a word is enough. An unexpected visit, with all these examples with family love we also learn to love and cherish our boyfriends, friends, etc. We know that it is normal to know each other before starting a relationship as boyfriend and girlfriend, and decide if that person can be a spouse, of course the father of your children. Right?

But now many things have changed, we know that we also have children out of wedlock; that's why we have so much insecurity, generations after generations. When we feel a little bit of that love that maybe we never had, we don't feel it.

We think twice to get involved in things that we do not know if it is something real or if with them, we are going to suffer even more. Things that we do not think now of feeling loved, wanted, or pampered. It is so much so that sometimes we see visions, we believe we are loved when that person is also confused and does not know what he/she wants. It is possible that at that moment they need to believe in someone, it turns out that it will not be for a long time, the opposite will happen.

We must understand that love does not come to us so easily, it must be built little by little, not only with words but with deeds, nor does it have to be with exchanges. For example, you give me something and I give you something; no, it cannot be rotating. When it comes to a couple, each one must demonstrate their own 50% in the relationship, here you can see the difference.

But the question is, will today's couples give 50%? We do not know that, what is certain is that when couples are unequal, one has to understand that there may be many expectations or demands, because beforehand we know that if that person has the ability to make their partner happy, and even if they are not prepared or skilled as it should be, when you love your partner very much is in you to sacrifice yourself and show that you can love that person if you want him/her with you. Then your partner begins to value you and love you more. Sometimes we think that they have to love us for being beautiful, that is the biggest mistake, beauty has to be accompanied by everything that implies love, it should be noted that elegance helps a lot, but it is necessary that you decorate it with the companions, such as respect, solidarity and above all intelligence that is what will lead to achieve what you need to cover all those insecurities that surround both the man and the woman.

To have insecurity means to have lack of love for oneself and to be afraid to love others. Since you must love yourself first and then love others. When you love others without them loving you, that love will never be complete, since you will realize that you have no hope, you are just living in the moment, and at any moment it can end. It is when you despise believing in your mind that you are not important, that you are not wanted and that maybe you have some defect, that is not true, it is just as we mentioned before; you must love yourself first.

Example:
In true love and friendship you must be a little careful. They say that "friend is a buck in your pocket," they say that because when you go out with a friend, if you don't have money, they don't look at you the same way, it's a shame to act like that, we have no right to do it, even more if the luck of having money goes with us. But friendship is when you show your loyalty in the moment of need, when they take care of you and support you when you need it the most. Always try to get to know your friends well and deeply to avoid disappointments that could end any kind of friendship you consider having.

Love comes easy

Experience: in my case, I feel that my children are the love that fills my life. Thanks to Jamaine for being my son and for being the person he is, thanks to Justin for being my son and for valuing his family, thanks to Yaosmel for helping me to be a better mother, helping me to fly, bringing a lot of joy, hope to keep fighting in life, and being the biggest push which filled me with a new life, when I felt like dying, because of the disappointments, stumbles, and sufferings.

With your arrival I felt renewed, ready to start again with my God, who has given me that light and look through all the adversities, letting me know that love for my neighbor is what leads us to wash away so many negative impurities and feel alive in body and soul, but above all the soul. When the soul is filled with joy, the body functions at a positive rhythm that feels like an 89% turnaround in your life, compared to 10% before. It is as if you were born again, that experience I can tell you at this moment of my life, because previously I felt that nothing was nothing, everything was the same to me, I did not value the things around me.

It took me a lot to get it, but everything became insignificant. To the point that I did not love myself, I did not dress up and I did not want to live as before, it felt very unpleasant, that lack of love for everything, it was practically as if I did not exist in the world and from one moment to another little by little everything was changing when I had an encounter with God, and I spoke to him with my heart giving all my life and everything that was around me, I felt that I could no longer continue, I had no energy to continue fighting. Thank you, Lord, because you did the work with me, after talking to you, you gave me the love that I needed so that life would continue, that the love that I did not have would multiply, that all the things that I did not value would be reminder objects of what I was before. For that reason, I could not falter, to think that I always loved myself, and others. I just didn't see it at that moment, my God enlightened me and cleansed my sight and my soul so I could see all those obscurities in which, one gets confused, and one believes that love has never arrived and, it has always been there, it is just that we lose communication with God and the negative spirit makes one see otherwise. Love does not come so easily, but it is an immense force that moves and stirs even the dullest of a flame, just think of those hugs when someone rushes towards you, thanks you, serves you and when you can serve another.

It is like having a favorite plate of food on the table and you eat it so eagerly, with the difference that the next day you digest the food but when you serve and give love it is forever, there is nothing more beautiful than that feeling of seeing hope in our faces, that we could make a difference.

I realized it because, in the midst of so many problems I had in mind, it was almost like when a television is damaged and you can only see white noise, that was my case; but the funny thing was that instead of thinking about solving all those problems I had, although I had no idea how to solve them, I thought about how to make a change in pregnant and confused women, adults, old people who had no place to live, abandoned children, every night I thought about how I could make a difference in the lives of these people and bring a smile on their faces.

But I knew that only love, my beliefs, and the need to see those smiles on those sad faces, that sometimes they do not know if love exists, and that with time they will realize if there was a change or not in the lives of these people.

Justin Ortiz

Justin is my second son. A very passionate boy doing what he loves, for me he is a blessing. On the other hand, when he was little, we all thought he was going to be a person not able to make his own decisions, I could tell he was very restless, he couldn't concentrate. Then the doctors diagnosed him with ADHD. I always had to look for him at school, because the teachers couldn't deal with him, they also prescribed him medications that made him dizzy and completely without energy, like he was another person. As a mother I did not agree with those treatments, from the beginning I saw how my son walked like a zombie, with his mind far away, it broke my heart to see him like that and I started to think how I could change that condition and treat him without medication. I thought that over time it could cause him more damage. I thought that when he reached adulthood, he might feel less capable than others, so I decided not to give him medication. When he was little it was a little difficult for me since I had to pick him up from school because of his restlessness when he couldn't concentrate. When I couldn't leave work, I had to call someone else to pick him up, so I felt like I had to do something. I started to do many activities and try to tire him out after school, bathing him with cold water and at the same time boiling a chamomile tea, letting it cool down and putting it on his head, drying him with a towel and going to bed with him, giving him lots of kisses, sometimes singing to him and he would fall asleep peacefully. That's how I treated him, little by little I was able to take him off those medications. I know that many parents are going through the same thing, I just want them to know that medication is not the solution to the problem. But at the end of the day, as a parent, we are the ones who must be with our children all their lives. I thank God because to this day he is very intelligent, disciplined, respectful, a very good son, a person with a very positive attitude. He is a good worker every day. Justin thank you for being the way you are.

JUSTIN

Justin & Mom

Family

Family is the most beautiful thing you can have, family is not only having children, father, mother, siblings, but also the people who care about you. Those people who are not blood relatives, sometimes behave better than your own family members. The thing is that no matter what problems we have, when it comes to family, there is no greater satisfaction than their company and support. In some of the cases many families are evicted, have moved from one place to another, live in other countries, and it is very difficult when they live far apart, it can take years to see each other.

Many wish to see each other for a moment, that is why when you can have your family, you must take advantage of it, love it, value it, let it spoil you and know that everyone needs to have a family. If you can have it, you must know how to value it, and teach other family members its importance; for example, there are many ways to show love to family, no matter the distance, we can have communication through different ways, telephone, letters, social networks, etc.

There are many thoughtful details one can offer to the family to keep them close and to let them know how much we love them. There was a case that I saw up close, for example, a daughter of 10 siblings who worked 70 hours a week, to be able to buy a house for her mother and younger siblings. In addition, we also had to consider that she was a single mother of two children, it was very difficult, but she achieved what she wanted to do so much for her mother and her younger siblings. They never lost that love and desire to get back together, and the father and mother were also able to be together on behalf of the siblings. Even on holidays there are many ways to keep the family together, it doesn't matter if you don't have money, even if you are poor, when there are family ties, you can still be together.

The only way to complete true love and if, unfortunately, one of them is lost, you feel that you've lost your life.

My third pregnancy

Being a mother for the third time was something I wanted, but when it happened, I didn't expect it. My youngest son was 11 years old, being a mother for the third time was like being a mother for the first time. Unfortunately, I was a single mother, something different than I had expected. Since my excitement of being a mother again, was for us to live together for a long time and enjoy the pregnancy as a couple.

Every night I would ask myself why it was like this, I would just talk to God, and tell him that he was the father of my child. Because for some reasons, I did not feel the true love of the father of my child, I do not blame him because I felt responsible for everything. That gave me strength to continue, even if I was sad. When my baby was moving in my belly that insecurity, anxiety, and helplessness meant nothing, because at that moment it was the only thing I had, and it was with me. My children were my hope, happiness, and a breath of tenderness.

Many negative things were always going through my head, confusions that made me make drastic decisions, but in the end, I always stayed in the same circle. I didn't know if it was going to be a boy or a girl, but my mind told me it was going to be a boy. A friend and I started looking for names and we decided that it was going to be called Yaosmel, the name for me meant that the child was mine alone, having a unique name.

Despite having many things on my mind, I was always thinking about my first two children. I decided to write this topic in honor of mothers who have gone through the same thing, since we always want to know what each of us feel when similar situations happen to us; at the same time, they are beautiful but difficult. We women dream of having stability and being happy with our family by our side.

To have access to all your cravings, but above all to have a happy pregnancy; to not have stress, worries, that lead you to depression which is not good. In my situation, I remember that I used to request for God's help in a great way, to give me strength to go on, because sometimes I felt that I was losing all my energy. At that moment something very strange happened, my legs were bent when I was writing this topic and at that moment, I closed my eyes and I felt that my legs were straight again, I could hear a voice through my thoughts, that told me:

Don't worry I know who you are, this is not a punishment, I believe it is a reward, I more than anyone else know what you have been through and the anguish in your heart. This is just a stage in your life which will only bring you happiness and achievements along the way, your projects will flourish. Do not see life through others, but, through your capacity, you can achieve and prove that there is no negativity, and if there is, you can turn the negative into something positive. You will see that all your anxieties and worries will be words that will only cause you laughter when you remember them. Above all, don't blame yourself, don't judge yourself before being evaluated.

Because many of us believe that we are alone, but our Lord Jesus is always watching over us.

Yaosmel   Rodríguez

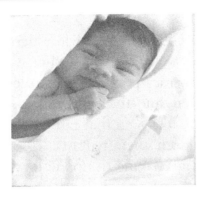

Yaosmel   Rodríguez
August 9, 2011, at 2:27 pm
6 pounds, 12 ounces 19.5 inches
With love, Inmacualada

35

Father and children

Father and children sound like perfect and beautiful words. It is wonderful to have a father, to have children is even greater. Both sides play different roles, the father must support his children, and the child must obey their parents, although nowadays it is seen that fathers do not respect their children, nor children their parents. If only we knew the importance of always having our parents with us, feeling that love and support that we need so much.

Many have them and do not give them the necessary importance, they do not value them, they do not know the love that parents have for their children, but we only realize it when we no longer have them. Then, it is there where we are regretting the things, we did not do for them when we had them by our side, our conscience does not leave us alone and we start to say or try to do different things. Children are the most important thing one can have, as if they were the most precious treasure, one takes care of them, pampers them, and wants to free them from anything that may happen to them.

Unfortunately, children are borrowed, one can have them to a certain extent. The good thing is that in some cases there are children who never want to leave their parents' side, it is nice, and that is why we want to take care of them, because they want to be taken care of by their parents. On the other hand, it is because they have not yet become independent, but many parents find it funny, since some parents have only one child, unlike others who have 5 or even 10. I knew a family that had 13 children and they were very poor; as parents, they did what they could, but there was a time when things got difficult for them, they wanted a better future for their children. Unfortunately, in the place where they lived it was impossible, they had to make very complicated decisions. The parents were forced to look for families with a better economic position to give away part of their children, it was very difficult, but they had to think about the future of those children, so that they would have what they needed.

The parents decided to let go of their family little by little, the good thing was that the families they gave their children to were recommended by other families who had already done the same. The parents had the opportunity to visit whenever they wanted, which kept them close to their children and aware of their children's progress. As time went by, some of the children improved and became independent one by one; the story of this family was beautiful since the children bought a house in the city in a short time and the whole family was together again.

They did not forget each other, and thanked God for everything they had achieved, and for having their parents again. The siblings were the happiest, they could finally be with their parents, and the brothers and sisters shared as if they had never been separated; this confirms the importance of the family, of course, the children never forgot the beings that brought them to the world, and never stopped fighting so that their family could share the most beautiful thing that is family unity, brotherly love, and the love of the children for their parents. We could say what a beautiful family, and what a beautiful effort they made so that the family ties would not be broken. To this day, they are still in contact with the families that adopted them, and they are all still together with many grandchildren and get along very well.

Prisoner in the United States

When you live in the United States, whether it is for one year or ten years, it never crosses your mind that you may go to jail. Like many immigrants, when we are in the United States, we want to get rich overnight, either because we left poor families back home or because we want to impress others, and sometimes we do not measure the consequences.

We should dedicate ourselves to earn the money honestly, but we start to generate ideas, without knowing who is watching us, we get the taste of acquiring things the easy way, without thinking about the risks, for example, illegal jobs, it is yourself that is sinking in the void. In those moments you don't care about the consequences because you are getting a lot of money. We human beings, feel that we are in the glory, we think we own everything that surrounds us. the bad thing is when you have no way out; then that's when the regrets come, you say: *"if I had never done all these bad things, my life would be different."*

Unfortunately, it is already too late, and we practically say that we have two options; of those two, we don't know which one we are going to choose, either we go to our country escaping from justice or we are willing to serve our sentence. Sentence after being served, ends in deportation. In those moments is when you lose your emotional life with your friends, family and children, the privileges you had before. Being deprived of your freedom is the hardest thing a human being could go through. Even if they detain you where you are living, or transfer you to another state, it can take hours or days for someone to come and see you. It was difficult for us family members to visit our loved ones who, because of their own mistakes, are in this situation. It is important to let them know that no one must criticize anyone, and that everyone is there for a reason. We live a difficult life being imprisoned, so that someone else can make it more difficult. Most people see things differently. We tend to judge everybody, and we hold resentment towards the person who made the mistake. It is nice to be able to give without expecting to receive anything in return, things that most people who are imprisoned are not used to. Sometimes ignorance becomes a bit intolerant and that leads us to make many mistakes.

No matter how small or big things are, I repeat, everyone is in prison for some reason. There was a prisoner who was arguing with another one; one of them started to say inappropriate words, saying that he was there for something very stupid, the other prisoner answered: *"you are right, I am here for stealing 5 million dollars, on the other hand, you are here for having sold drugs, I prefer to have stolen my millions than to be killing people in the street."* Then the other prisoner began to think about the harm he was doing to human beings.

Now he is going through the worst moments of his life, but we must understand that we are human beings, that we are exposed to many temptations, complicity, vices, and competitions. We take refuge in getting easy money and making up for the problems and needs we have, but when we are in prison we don't think about those things. For my part, I have learned and observed how difficult the process is that one must go through and get used to all the rules when we are in prison. The first thing is that you are going to be sharing with different nationalities who of course are not all imprisoned for the same thing, in the same way you will meet selfish and envious people who don't care about anything. People who, instead of changing, become cold, calculating, and inhuman, you feel like you are living in a pen of wild animals, with no way out, no hope, but you must do the time anyway. Many of us have no faith, some of us would go to churches asking God to get us out of there. Sometimes they themselves ended up saying; it is good that God put me in this place because through the circumstances I recognize things that they did not understand before or it is possible that something worse would have happened to me outside. After such a strong experience is that they understand that they were good people, as well as that for everything that they went through, there are consequences and that they needed to change to be a good example in society.

A reason to continue

After living a moment as intense as a divorce, loss of a job, loss of your children, etc., not because God has taken it away, but because in many cases when you get divorced it is not only a divorce where the wife is willing and the husband does not agree, there are usually many contradictions, especially regarding the custody of the children, in my case, my life was destroyed because the lies seemed truths in front of a judge, and when someone with more experience manages to wrap and confuse many things, you may or may not win the battle, many people get depressed and remain so destroyed that after a while they do not know where they stand.

But in my case, my motivation was my children, the strange thing is that the judge gave temporary custody to the father. My love as a mother made my two children be the reason for me to never stop. I knew that sooner or later I was going to have them back. Nevertheless, I could not believe that because I took my children on vacation to my native country, where my mother lived, my husband was going to go to the judge to formulate 1000 stories saying that the children were going to leave the country without his consent, that they were not going to return to the United States.

Of course, it was all a lie because their mother had bought round trip tickets, so there was no problem, so I did not understand the appointment I received to go to court and I decided to ask the children's father, who told me, do not worry, forget it, you do not have to go, I thought you were going to leave them with your mother, forget about going to court. So, I did, I never went to court, then, a few days passed, and I received another letter from the court saying that the father had temporary custody. I, Almita, could not believe what was happening, I almost went crazy and could not understand it, because the children's father showed up with some policemen to pick them up and take them to his house, at that time we had been married for five years, I never believed him capable of something so cruel, like separating me from my children, deceiving the judge in that way, as a woman

I tried to take it easy, since I had to work to pay him child support, for me it was a real drain, and to top it all off, he spent the money on alcohol and other vices; I decided to look for a lawyer, he could never do anything, it was to get permanent custody back and divorce, he would always tell me a long story, every time I went to court, the case became more and more complicated, 10 years of suffering passed, then, God began to do justice, the man began to get sick and ended up in the hospital, until in one of these relapses he suffered a heart attack that had left him half immobile.

It was he himself who told me that he could no longer take care of the children, that he had no time to take care of himself, much less others. So, I went back to court explaining the situation and they gave me back my children and approved the divorce, it was like being born again, because it was like ending that nightmare that lasted many years before it could be resolved. I kept fighting, working to give a healthier life to my children and trying to forget everything they suffered when they were little.

So far, a little time has passed, and I achieved the dream of being together with the children again and now they are all very happy. After all this, I got married again, got pregnant, and everyone is happy with the new baby, it is a blessing. God changed everyone's life and all around us. With the new pregnancy even those who were not family were giving us a lot of support, to the point that I felt as if I had been the first pregnant woman in the world, they made me feel that way, they were looking for all my likes, my cravings; and for me it was a dream come true, since after 11 years of not having children, I thought I was going to have a lot of criticism from everyone.

Open Hearted

Open-hearted is when you open your heart to others and let yourself be loved. You can love and everything you do should be with love, with your friends, family, children, neighbors, and everything around you. There are many people who do many charitable works. And many institutions that receive donations and despite receiving them, they also end up donating part of their things. Many celebrities donate a lot of money for different aid programs. Despite all this help seems not to end all the needs that we have around the world. And we know that it is not only about one person, but also the responsibility of the president of each country, not to let humanity suffer the way it suffers.

Open heartedness also means making campaign groups in which all needs are addressed and fighting for what we deserve. For the time being, we know that we do not have to be artists or presidents to do our part in making our needs known, we know that there are many, but the most important is health and it must do a lot with drinking water, and how we can help our community, giving them hope and encouragement and above all be consistent with oneself.

Interpretation

Open heart helps our first and second generation, in which we discipline and educate, of course our children will be better parents and with an open heart to help and be helped.

Friends

They are very important people in our lives because we trust them with some of our secrets. Sometimes, we even think that they are part of our family. There is nothing wrong with that, as we often don't have family, and friends become family. It's good to have someone to confide in, to cry with, and to listen to you.

But be careful, no matter how close they are, you can't fully trust them. Sometimes you think they are a friend, but they are a buck in your pocket; as the saying goes, "he who has nothing is worth nothing." This means that sometimes there are many friends who are with you because of what you have or what you can give them, and not because they are happy to share difficult moments with you. The worst thing is that these types of friends act very cunningly for fear of being found out. They don't want to lose you as a friend because of some benefits they can get from you. Many let it show and others let it go, believing that these people are like that, but these friends disguise themselves with many faces and act different roles to confuse you. The good thing is that since they are not real actors, sooner or later they end up making mistakes and uncovering the lie. That's when you find out what kind of friend you had, leaving you in deep pain as you learn about everything you trusted that supposed friend who was never really a friend. Chances are that everything they know about you, many other people know about you as well. Not to mention that they can steal from you and even take your partner away from you. Many are envious, they can't stand the fact that they have nothing and someone else can have everything.

Scene:

Miguelina had a friend for 10 years, she was like her sister, they all did it together; What do we do together? The only thing missing was that the husband shared. Everything was extremely calculated, and those 10 years ago, the friend's plan was to kill her little by little so that she would remain with her grandma's fortune. Miguelina suffered from asthma, so it was easy to provoke an asthma attack. She used addictive powders so that Miguelina died easily and silently, so that it seemed like a natural attack. In those 10 years, the friend was gaining ground, since when Miguelina died, she could also stay with her husband and inheritance. The couple didn't have children, it was a little easier for her to confess her poisonous strategies to her husband. Until Miguelina finally died of an asthma attack and her supposed friend managed to stay with everything, her husband and all her heritage. Later, the husband of the deceased discovered his friend's macabre plan. Fortunately, he was able to find incriminating proof and manage to put them in jail.

Interpretation:

It is important not to get carried away by appearances, much less vent with just anyone. And if someone shows you that they only want to be with you for what you have, they are not your friend. It is difficult to spot the signs, but sometimes many will act cautiously to confuse their victims, so it is best to rely on your mother or a pastor when you want to talk about your family problems, that we at least know that there is more confidentiality, when it comes to our secrets or something that bothers us. It is very sad to realize that after having many years of trusting a friend, the disappointment can be fatal or decisive, as we have seen many cases of death.

Wedding

When I mention wedding, it means happiness or decisions already taken. As we all know, there are rich and poor weddings. When we talk about a poor wedding, it doesn't even come close to the rich wedding. But at the end of the day, rich or poor, they are all the same. The ceremony, the guests, the food, drink, and everything else. So, I wonder if there are unnecessary exceptions at times. Many people are happy doing it the way they think, even if they know they won't be happy for long. They take their chances no matter what happens later.

Sometimes women make the decision to get married early, just because of the obsession to put on the white dress and of course the curiosity of how it feels to be married, or rather we might think that we will find more mutual respect. I think you must keep in mind that it is better to live for a long time and get to know the person better. Even if you don't know the person completely you will have the satisfaction that, if the relationship ends, there is no need for a divorce, or frustration of time wasted in preparing for a wedding. The reason to take this into account, is because after a bad experience, when it is your turn to officially get married, your mind will be blocked with unresolved confusions. You may often disappoint your current partner.

Example of marital frustrations:
A girl named Maria. She was waiting a long time to get married. She had this desire to have a partner. In her case she already had children from her previous partner; but she had never married in a white dress. After waiting for more than 20 years, she found someone who she thought was the

perfect match. He was a person who loved to be at home. She didn't like to go out, but rather wanted to feel accompanied in the remaining years of her life. The time came and the date to get married. Maria did not care if they gave her material things, she just wanted to be married, she was going to live with her husband and by marrying him, she believed she was going to be very happy.

The wedding was over, and they went on their honeymoon. Maria did not live in the country where they were married. She had to travel from her country to her husband's country, since her husband could not travel. For him to be able to travel could take several years. Maria's whole family wondered what was the point of waiting 20 years to get married if they were not really going to live together? The relationship was not going to be the same. Practically the marriage was going to be over the phone; is that what we call Marriage? I don't think it's worth it.

Maria could not travel often to see him, since she had to wait for her vacation time to visit him. The boy got desperate and started dating other women. He did not respect his wife, Maria; whether it was because of the distance or because he was not mature enough to wait a little longer for Maria, we never knew. The marriage did not even last three months. Maria found out everything he was doing. She loved him very much, but he didn't want to admit the mistakes he had made. That's when she decided to file for divorce. Heartbroken by all the struggles and disappointments that were hard to overcome. Maria says she doesn't wish that bad experience on anyone, she felt an emptiness and pain in her heart. The only lesson she had left was not to fall again. Considering the family destruction that is difficult to recover.

Conclusion: Get to know the person well, even if you have never been married in your past life. Wait patiently because what is for you will be for you. In this life what starts fast, ends fast. It is better to live a quiet life, and don't suffer the deception of not being able to live to tell the tale.

Farewell letter

I had the opportunity to be in a spiritual retreat sharing with many women of different nationalities. I am Latina, it was very nice to meet all those women with different needs. They had different personalities. One day, they were one way, and, on another day, they would be so different. What I noticed most was the deep loneliness that did not seem to be filled. Companionship helps, but not to the point of total clinging. It's when parting comes that you really realize your feelings.

Letter:

For each of those women who were kind to me, I leave you a hug of remembrance. For those who acted indifferent, a prayer and God bless you forever. Those who were really with me through thick and thin, I wish them every blessing for all the things they offered me, even though I didn't need them. I hope God multiplies them three times for the good heart they had. But among so many women there was a very special one. There came a time when I was very hungry, she fed me, she listened when I told a colleague that I was hungry, and she knew I was pregnant. She approached me, offering me something to eat. It was such a beautiful thing for me, it caused me a lot of tenderness. I hope that God repays her for this gesture of tenderness that touched my heart; to see that there are still noble people. I hope you enjoy your blessings when you receive them. Thank you because your nationality is not mine, and however you behaved like a sister; what we call family. As they say, family is not necessarily someone with your same blood, but that one who is with you, listening and encouraging you. I say goodbye with the hope that all that we learned and put into practice will not be in vain. Blessings to all.

A letter to "love"

A letter to a love that I always wanted to have; no matter the adversities and the distance, because when love is true it doesn't matter how far away you are. The important thing is when that love passes you by, your body and your heart tremble, it's as if you were in a freezer. For that same reason I feel that if I were with you the way I want, I think I would be the happiest woman; in that same way I hope that this act of affection will make you the happiest man of this day.

I have learned that in life the only beautiful thing you can have, is the happiness you are living in the moment. I hope you know that this minute can be the time when you decide if you want, I will be waiting for you. Even if your decision is different; it doesn't change anything. The important thing is that on this day you feel happy, and that you enjoy everything that is around you. We know about today, but not about tomorrow. That's why I wanted to show you how happy you can be when you want to be, and I want to be happy with you.

With this I don't want to say that you should make hasty decisions, since everyone acts depending on their feelings. If yours are different from mine, in the same way if you are happy, I will also be happy with you, because I know you, and what I can see is that despite being together and at the same time separated, I feel that the few moments I share with you, are filled with happiness. I have also decided to respect your decisions, as well as being willing to listen to whatever you have to say, without being afraid of negative reactions, because thanks to God I have learned the bad things in life, but more importantly, I see all the good things. The best thing is to make everyone you love, happy. I feel that I love you, I feel your kisses, your caresses, and when you do it, I feel that you do it with love. For me that has a lot of value, although sometimes we act with indifference, I know that, in the bottom of our hearts, we keep something special. We only need to lose our fear and all the barriers that separate us; give ourselves a chance so that we can remember forever as something true and beautiful.

A letter to a sister in God

Hello sister, I didn't think I would find you, but you came and appeared to me like a barbie. You are a super beautiful and elegant woman, but what makes you more beautiful is your simplicity, it stands out in your face. Thank you for talking to me and for giving me the opportunity to meet you. After talking to you I could realize all your virtues, so I felt the need to tell you that all these virtues must continue to flourish. I was listening to your story, and in it, you say that you are not sure about having children.

It seemed to me that maybe you were denying yourself the opportunity to complete the happiness you deserve. I understand that we all have different thoughts. Some for circumstantial reasons, and others for reasons that are not understandable. As a sister in God, I can tell you that family is the most beautiful thing one can have, especially if it comes from you. That feeling when you see it and feel that it is yours, will not be able to compare with anything that you have already lived. I just wish you would give yourself the chance to someday remember me. I also hope that when that day comes, it will be one of the happiest moments of your life. Then you will realize that everything you do for others will have its deserved reward; by wanting to help your other siblings. This is a letter to a sister in God, who was denied those feelings since she was a little girl, as she, now feels the need to let her know the importance of having someone, like our children, who are considered a gift from God.

Conformity

Conformity means to survive with the little we can get. For example, if we have one or two changes of clothes, we already know that we must wash them, over-wash them to wear them every day. Just as if we have one pair of shoes, that is the one we will wear for all occasions. If we don't have enough to eat, we make do with what we have at that moment. These are simple examples, but when one does not have the facilities to live around everything necessary, we must make do with what we have in hand. Unless we decide to get things the hard way, and then pay the consequences. I mean that many times we kill, steal, and envy others.

That doesn't mean we have to be conformists all the time. It just means that we need to know that we must work more according to what God wants. That way we can have everything we need. Understand that the most important thing is to have a home and that there is peace in our family. When there is love in a home, we can say that we have everything. But sometimes we don't value those things, we think that because they are around us, we don't need them. When we don't have them anymore, is when we realize the true value of what we had. Then we say, we no longer need clothes, shoes, or anything material. We only want what really makes us happy, of course, family. Because if we don't care about our own blood, it's as if one didn't love oneself.

Scene:
This was a very powerful family with a lot of money; they didn't care about anything, they had everything. They had mansions, land, cars, businesses and millions and millions of dollars. But this family didn't even give importance to all those material things because it was very easy for them to get

everything and many more things. Eventually they lost everything they had, because even though they obtained things easily, they didn't share it. This family was not doing things right. When they lost everything, they had to conform with the little they had left; but they did learn to value their family and no longer cared about material things. They said that the only thing that mattered to them was having enough to eat.

Interpretation:

It is ironic to have to lose everything to recognize that conformity does not mean having nothing; but valuing the much and the little we have. Strive to be at peace with yourself. That will lead you to have enough for you and yours. Because our Lord does not like us to live in lack, He always provides enough for us to be happy. This is a test for us to understand that we are born with nothing, and we die with nothing. When we get things that we can share, it will fill us with many more things. Especially spiritually. Many times, we feel empty, we do not understand why sometimes we have so much, and we do not have enough time to spend and enjoy. What good is it to have so much, because at the same time it is like having nothing.

The key to success and power: let others laugh and enjoy what they have achieved with their effort. And that is what will give you the key to human power that we all should have, they are keys that would open the heart of every human being, remember a smile brings another smile.

Believing to be happy

We all think that happiness is being rich or having money. But we are totally wrong. It is true that it helps a lot but when you have it, you realize that you need other things. You look around you and you feel that there is an emptiness. In my case, I was able to discover that what made me happy was to achieve my projects and goals, and to share with my family. Because, even if we are not rich, it is important to achieve all those things that lead to happiness.

As human beings, I think that one thing leads to another, if they are well thought out, analyzed, and shared with the people around us. Sometimes we think that having material things will make us happy, unfortunately it is not so. You can be happy for a moment, but you still feel that same emptiness inside you. I mean, there are going to be days when you are going to wish you didn't have money, that's just the way things are in life. Being happy doesn't necessarily have to come from material things. There are many ways to not feel empty. But we must find out, what really makes us happy, we are all different. The message is that priorities are to complete the intensity of the feelings of human beings.

Decisions

When it comes to decisions it is something very complicated, because when you make them, it is difficult to back out. Many times, decisions are made because we live blindly in the present, and for some reason or another God gives us the time to think and recover our lost memory. When I decided to write this topic, I had goose bumps and a racing heart, thinking that many of us are going through the same thing, compared to the present it is as if we were born blind in nature and waking up. It is as if we fell from a fifth floor and broke all our bones.

That's how we felt when we discovered what we were living. Sometimes we live in such dark relationships, and we don't realize it at the time, in our mind everything seems to be fine. Living in relationships of alcoholism, vices, from spouses, or close relatives. Apart from that we suffer inside, and we sacrifice ourselves so that things can be fixed, but we realize that it is impossible. That is when you suffer more and more, in many cases we must swallow it.

The sad thing is to wake up in a place where we are still struggling with the past, in a few words we are far from the memories but unfortunately, they come together with the present. It is so much what torments us that we want to turn it into the past and never remember them, but the most terrifying thing is when there are children involved and the support of your family is not present, that is when we make drastic decisions that although they hurt us in the deepest part of our heart we must fight against the current. It is not so easy to judge because nobody is perfect. To my understanding, when you love someone and you want to make a difference, you sacrifice yourself and do what is beyond your reach to make someone else happy, especially if you have made a promise and you want to give them a chance. Sometimes it is preferable to make decisions that even if it feels like our chest is burning in a flame, the best we can do is to leave things in the past. Sometimes we have no idea how to keep something positive to help us stay alive. The only thing that keeps us alive, are illusions, that although they are not real, they are only mental illusions to forget us in that moment of so much sadness.

The truth is that even if they are not real, they are only mental illusions to make us forget at that moment of so much sadness. The truth is that when we look around us, we realize that even the lowest people become our family.

Interpretation:

Before writing this topic, it was difficult but just as I also made decisions, at that moment I freed myself and cleaned myself inside, I no longer thought so much about the things that hurt me. For me it was like starting over. When one suffers so much in life and continues to be in the same situation, eventually, there is nothing you can believe in. Only God gives me peace and strength to continue, afterwards, the only thing that made me feel good, was to make the decision to have my third child, and now, that is my motivation to continue living.

Disillusions

We live a life of disappointments, of course if we look at it in a negative way, that will make us feel devastated; we all know that this feeling is one of the most common things that we as human beings go through daily. Since most of us believe that everything must be true and perfect. Regularly every human being does several things every day, they can be many, in all of them we will realize that some will not go well, that's why we say: What a Disappointment! We do not want to do them again and we end up angry with everyone around us; but there is also another kind of disappointment, those of couples, some plans we have for the future, do not go well.

When you start with that mental depression and frustration, you lose the will to live, that is when we have to be strong, of course not everyone can assimilate in the same way: but if it helps a lot to believe in yourself, and think that even if things do not go well that does not mean that all things will go wrong; they say that he who perseveres, succeeds.

I am going to tell you a story that is based on true facts and has to do with a disappointment. There was a girl named Berta, she was very active, she always liked to do things by her own effort, and she was a hard worker. She was also a good sister, a good mother, and a good friend, super enterprising. At that time, she was single for a year or two. She had been divorced and was struggling alone with her children, and as time went by, she suddenly received a phone call. A call she did not expect, and at the same time she never imagined the impact it would have on her, she was surprised because the caller was as if God had sent him. Her body warmed up, her eyes reddened, that is, she felt that at that moment she thought that she was talking to someone she already really knew. The funny thing is that the young man felt that way too. They kept talking, they felt chemistry immediately. The tone of voice of the young man was impressive, super elegant, sexy, and manly. Personally, as well as professionally, anyhow, Berta fell in love, practically over the phone. And as time went by, they became sweethearts, and formed a very nice relationship, by the way, so nice that the relationship lasted almost 10 years approximately. At that time the relationship was long distance, he lived in California, and she lived in New England, but despite the distance, Berta was still excited, and they respected each other, she focused more on him, because he was a very hardworking and simple person.

Berta was not a materialistic person, for her, things that have a measured value did not matter. She continued to fight for the relationship by talking to him, every day with excitement. And then she decided to travel to California to see him and he also came to see her. For Berta he was her prince charming, and she was trying very hard to make the relationship work. They already had 6 or 8 years of sharing together, there was never any negativity from him, he was always positive. Well, a little bit of time went by where it came to the final point of making decisions, whether to buy a house or not, and deciding to get married, that included him having to move from California to New England.

Make a life together and get ahead. And with all those decisions, there was no turning back for Berta, she was very excited with the many plans, very happy and after a week she had moved into a new house. At that moment she received a call from Prince Charming, saying that he no longer wanted to move to New England. He said, I don't like that city, I don't like the people, I don't think I could live there. I feel like I'm too used to my hometown, Berta I'm sorry. It was as if Berta was hit with a bucket of hot water, instead of cold water, but she listened very calmly and patiently, at the same time thinking about all the plans they had together and how she was going to be alone, because the decision to buy a house was for them to live together. At that moment everything fell apart, and she woke up from the scare and started to think when she was surviving alone with her children, it was a little different, she was used to being alone. But things between two people are easier.

In the end she was calm, she took it calmly and understood the decisions he made, but at the same time she moved on. Then she said: What a disappointment! To think that the person she knew for 8 years, did not fulfill the expectations as she thought he was, with a disappointment of that level, you must be very strong to move forward and not let yourself fall. So far Berta continues with her normal life, keeping her house and family with many plans; if we all saw things like Berta, we would not have disappointments; we would have the ability to resolve in a positive way, we would be practical and look for options and say: if you fall, you get up.

Discipline and respect

Discipline is something very nice when you get it, but also difficult to acquire, it is learned daily, especially when we are small, if we are polite, we have respect for others and when we combine it with sympathy, we will have open doors. In most cases both men and women do not need to have a virgin face or a spectacular body, by having discipline we will gather up to 85% of natural beauty that everyone loves, it is something that is contagious, and that we all would like to have. It is like a profession where we demonstrate our ability in any type of situation that arises.

The motivation before writing this topic is to make it clear that discipline is obtained by observing others. It is seen a lot in the pews, in the church, as well as in public places we see different disciplinary situations, in that instant we must act and give our example doing the right thing in front of others, the difference will be noticed, we will avoid discussions and misunderstandings, many times we get enemies for insignificant things.

When you analyze yourself, you know that you will always have an instinct before acting towards any bad reaction, in which you can feel sorry. Examples of the main acts of discipline, is to let yourself be noticed and show that you are not the same as others. If you want to talk to someone first knock on the door, if this person is busy wait for them to finish, when someone is talking wait for them to finish talking, until then introduce yourself.

Milly: Mr. Rafael, do you have a minute for me?
Rafael: Yes, Miss, how can I help you?

Milly: I wanted to know if I can have an advance on my salary.
Rafael: If I could know what the urgency is?

Milly: Yes, Mr. Rafael, I need to pay for college.

Using a little discipline and respectfulness it is possible that you can get something positive out of anything you want to get in life and life becomes easier. And you will see the difference if you act disrespectfully and don't know how to wait. For me personally, it bothers me a lot when I'm having a conversation with someone and someone else comes and interrupts. Also, when you are talking about an important topic with a friend, and they change the subject at any moment and don't let you finish your thought.

Another thing is that many people act as if they are not listening to you. When you act with that bad discipline you immediately make yourself known, and people are not going to take you into account and little by little they will move away from you, you will not even realize that those are one of the things that you can change, until you get used to it. Among other things within the daily discipline, you will gradually learn over time and your way of life will make human sense. By understanding and demonstrating that you are a human being just like everyone else.

Divorce

Divorce can be in some cases a relief, as well as a disaster. Sometimes we feel relief because when a couple divorces by mutual consent, there is less suffering on both sides. When children are involved, they will suffer as well. Disastrous divorces include many things; for example, not wanting to share assets, fights over child custody. All of these are devastating situations. Since a divorce can take time because some of them want to rebuild their life with another partner, even if they are still married. It's super stressful because it's like having double worries.

In general, divorces leave a lot of marks. That's when the regrets come, but unfortunately, it's late when we've been married for several years. We start complaining that we wasted our time, we suffer a lot, and we say, "we should never have married that person". We should not think like that; the truth is that in a marriage there can be many kinds of benefits. For example, modifying your personality and raising children under a marriage. It is important to set an example for the second generation, so that those children can raise their own children.

So, on and on we go to the point of divorce, you can save yourself and you can also sink. We say this because as they say out there, desperation is part of failure. Sometimes we think we have found our prince charming or princess, but the truth is that we suddenly find ourselves with the devil himself. All that you fought and wore yourself out to have a perfect marriage, was nothing more than a total loss, because during that marriage time, we may discover that the real prince charming was circling our bones and we, not even knowing it.

We have some examples of things that can happen in divorces. It may be that neither of you gets to keep the children and must hand them over to a family member. If they have no family, then the government takes care of them. The hard part is to get them back and everything becomes a nightmare that no one wants to live.

Another example of how a marriage can end is when they make a mistake and end up in jail. There are many people who get used to the system and do not have many options; because there are many years that they are doing in jail, and they must surrender themselves. Sometimes they give you the opportunity to discipline yourself, but for some people who must do a lot of time, the discipline stays there. They can't even employ what they learned on the outside because they are doing 20 to 30 years in prison. By the time they get out they are already old people, they don't have the strength to keep fighting.

In other cases, there are people who only must do 10 months or a year and end up being grateful for having been there, even if the punishment is small. Mistakes can be fatal no matter how small the mistake is and sometimes they turn into big things. They end up doing their punishment so that those crazy ideas that run through their mind can be changed. You must learn to value the things that you have out there no matter how simple they are. Those are the things that lead you to the greatest triumph, which is to maintain your marital union. You must learn to value your family and everything you have around you. Especially, in regards to the knowledge you had acquired in your life, it was just like a ghost, (every day you thought how you were going to be close to your loved ones), where there are only hopes, visions and dreams. Then, the days go by, but they don't seem to come to an end.

Sometimes you end up with a lot of moral and spiritual depression; but from my own experience I could say that you always must have faith. Ask our Lord. He hears everything we say and think. No matter how bad we have been. Think that things happen for a reason. That reason may be that we get to have a better life than the one we had before our bad experience. The good that is in store for us, in some of the cases, many women keep exploring and end up getting divorced quickly.

Others hold on because they have a family, since that is the most important thing. We need to recognize that we must fight and persevere with our partners. This is also how you get to the top. Many couples become happy in every way. It is difficult to get divorced and then having to start all over again. That doesn't mean that's going to be the solution to the problem. Since you don't know what you're going to run into. So as not to end up saying, "I left Guatemala to get into Guate-peor" (It means: Leaving a bad situation to get into something worse).
So, we keep trying and trying, until our life becomes a total confusion, where you don't even know what you want, and you harm yourself and your family.

The advisable thing to do is to be cautious. Make the best decisions that lead us to feel that we are alive, or on the contrary, to go through something worse, to feel like a ghost, trying to find the pieces that we think we have lost. It is in your hands to make the best decisions.

Pain

Pain is not an easy word. It can be defined in many ways, for example, pain of losing a child or a family member, pain of losing a love, loving someone and that person does not love you. Pain of separation from your loved ones, pain of little hope, all these similar pains can be happening to one person, and it does not come easy. And to think, how to remain standing with so much pain in your heart. Sometimes we go through pain, and we start going crazy and clueless.

And speaking of pain:

Oscarito was living all these pains, and he was still standing, working like crazy, getting up early and without any kind of depression, loving his wife more than ever and with plans. You also must understand that not all people are the same. Everyone cannot assimilate pain in the same way. It is better to try to fix the problem than to die in it, because there are pains that kill. There have been people who have killed for love, they could not bear to leave their partner, but we cannot judge those people who did it for different reasons.

They are difficult moments, there are people whose pain is so great that they cannot assimilate it, and they end up doing decisive things, such as death. Some do not die completely because they are saved in time, then the pain is double, because when they wake up from the coma, they start to remember everything and feel sorry, thanking God for being alive because for them it is like dying and being born again. They end up promising themselves to be a different person. The feeling of knowing that in a minute they were going to lose their life and their family. The most important thing Oscarito learned, that he survived all those pains together, and still had love for his family. The pains are invisible, without expecting it or deserving it, they originate, and they surface. And that's where there are so many questions that arise, we end up searching for answers, and in the end, we end up understanding the reasons why each one of us is going through it. Such strong pains are unbearable and difficult, to accept them at the same time is inexplicable. The truth is that we are humans, and we will all go through different situations. It is important to keep our feet on the ground, be realistic, and understand that there may be worse things that would no longer be pains but catastrophic and deadly   things.

The world of the living

We all know that we are born, we grow up, and we die. The world of the living is very complicated, in our minds we believe that we are not going to die. And we always act improvised as if we were immortal, and we don't think for a moment that any false step can make us disappear from the world of the living.

It doesn't matter if you are famous, rich, or poor, if you are fat or skinny, and so on. We also look at the fact that if we come from a long-lived family we always say: I am not going to die at an early age, because my grandparents are still alive. We should consider that our first generation was very careful, without addictions or any kind of vices. And if this first generation lasted 80 to 100 years, or 105 years, it means that they had a healthy life.

And our second generation if we would last 100 years, we may only reach 80; the third generation may have an exception, they may reach 70; it does not mean that they should die exactly at that age. Each of us can self-analyze and take care of ourselves, and we can lengthen our lives in a general sense. Thus, each of us could name the death of one of our family members and the reasons why they died. If we thought more and were more aware of the world of the living, we would not pass quickly into the world of the dead.

Example:
This is an example of a family that in less than 10 years lost different family members. They were a married couple, the brother of the wife of this couple of 10 children was like a son to her and stepbrother of children. Something unexpected happened, the man named Román had

disappeared for 5 days, and nobody knew where he was, they looked for him everywhere. The place where they lived was small, it was almost impossible for him to be in those surroundings. They decided to look for him in a distant farm, which is 40 minutes away from where they lived, they feared the worst. Because Mr. Román suffered from an illness called epilepsy. Unfortunately, they found him dead among the leaves and covered with ants, almost destroyed. All the neighbors managed to lift him up and put him in a coffin, so that Mr. Román could have a holy burial. But the family's pain was double, knowing that no one was there when he had an epileptic seizure, which could have saved him.

The final destiny for Mr. Roman was to die at 35 years of age, no one was around him. After 5 years, unfortunately another tragedy happened in his family, this time it was one of his 21-year-old sons, a young man with a complete life ahead of him, super intelligent and with a wonderful heart. He liked to help all his people, he was very good with his siblings, his parents, and his grandparents. He was the favorite grandson; his name was Jesus. He would go to visit his relatives, from the city to the countryside approximately two hours from where his parents and siblings lived.

Everyone remembers that the last visit was on a Sunday, after two weeks, Jesus went for a ride with his girlfriend, riding his bicycle to a city closer to where they lived, all laughing very happily. The party was over, and he was on his way back home in the evening. Suddenly, as if it were a scene from a movie or a mystery, a pickup truck appeared out of nowhere and ran over the motorcycle he was riding. By the way, his girlfriend died too, she was only 16 years old. It was very hard to believe that a young couple with a whole future ahead of them would die that way. It was devastating for the whole family and very difficult to recover.

These are facts of real life, that in comparison to the grandfather of that family who died at the age of 90, understand that for the world of the living there is no age to pass to the world of the dead. For us the living, never forget our dead relatives. In other words, we live between the living and the dead in a way, because the feelings of our loved ones never leave our souls and live in us. We must keep in mind that many of us are alive but our mind, or behavior towards others is dead. Remember if we are breathing and can move, we are in the world of the living. It is important to act as living beings.

He who has nothing is worth nothing

Unfortunately, we always believe that if you have nothing you are worth nothing. In the world in which we live we see ourselves that way, but we have good news, if it were that way the world would not exist for those who have nothing, maybe those people have more than any rich person we see out there, we say it this way because there are poor people who want to pretend to be rich, demonstrating and showing what they have, for that reason many think that the one who has nothing is worth nothing, and they focus and think that they will be rejected by others.
- "We should be cautious with the people we have around us because we do not believe in those who have nothing."-

We should not be with that kind of people, because, even if you have, the day you don't, people will throw you aside and you will end up suffering for something that is not worth it. That doesn't mean that your friend must be humble like you, if not at least have good feelings, and not look at you in a different way just because you don't have anything. In many cases there are people who have had nothing, and the luck of their life comes to them, and they still act as if they have nothing, it's a nice thing because they remember the life they had before.

Scene:
Kaioska: She was a young and pretty girl with many attributes; she grew up in different environments, with rich people, poor people, and even with people who had nothing to eat.
Kaioska was a special person, she was never inclined to share with wealthy people, even though the boys who sought her,

72

were people with money, she did not care about any of that, what really mattered to her were the people who suffered for not having anything to feed their children. But at the same time Kaioska could not do anything for these people, she was only 15 years old, she was training for a future, and she always said my God how much she wished she had to help these people, what a satisfaction I would have been able to give smiles to all of them, and at the same time I understood that there were many people who could help, and did nothing. In this case, practically every man for himself; if you stop for a moment to think, if God gave you enough to eat, why not help your neighbor, that way our creator can provide more, but unfortunately many people do not do it, knowing that next to you there are many hungry children, and we do not care if they need something.

Scene:

Kaioska: she never forgot about all those people, but at the same time she knew that they were going to see many families with many needs. Kaioska got lucky and got some money. And the first thing she had in mind was to open a center, for all the children in the neighborhood, where they would go to eat. And so, she could bring a little happiness to all those families who had nothing. They were the saddest people for not having anything, but it was worse was that they couldn't even provide food for their children.

Kaioska also opened a center for old people with disabilities, because in some countries they don't have the necessary benefits to survive, and they end up dying before their time. But this girl was very curious, she wanted to know if after 20 years, when she decided to return to her hometown, the people of the community were still the same; what she did know was that they had changed a little; Kioska decided to disguise herself as a poor person, she walked with a tied cloth and torn pants, and with old tennis shoes, she pretended to be another person, and tried to mingle with some people of the high class, that is to say wealthy people, she wanted to know their address. It is important to know that after 20 years one wants to believe that people are more civilized, more human, more compatible, and more vulnerable; not to believe that just because they have everything, they can take the world by the hand than another to see their reaction.

And the result was the same, they looked at her with different eyes, as if to say and this is where she came from, the companions looked from one side to the other seeing Kiaoska as if they felt ashamed of her; in those times of the test Kaioska was already doing her work with the children, and with people in need, but she did not want anyone to know that it came from her, she wanted to keep it a secret, because it was something that was making her very happy, so she did not have to let anyone know that it was her, the funny thing is that everyone wanted to know if it had been the president, the author of the works, or who was really in front of them, since there were many people talking about it and they were very happy about what was happening.

Well, the end of the test came, Kaioska made a press conference, to let them know the benefits that the project was going to leave, where all the beneficiaries were going to be present, and aware of the benefits. The project was a building with different floors to meet different needs. The architects presented the design together with the master builders for the end of the project. And the surprise they got when they saw Kaioska looking poor, they could not believe that she was the owner of the project. They all turned their heads, and looked at each other, because with a before and after Kaioska, the way she was dressed was totally different, but at the same time simple.

Observation:

The key to power and intensity in which something not visible or invisible is noticeable, you should not necessarily show what you have. Because what good is it to show what you have if you are not going to share it, better keep it to yourself and maybe you have the chance of not having guilty conscience, knowing that you could have done something and you did nothing. He who has nothing is worth nothing, is a theme inspired by a boy who suffered a lot, I mean material things, but he was a person with a lot of discipline, personality, desires, and consistency, but it must be emphasized that above all you must love yourself.

Emotions

There are different kinds of emotions, you can be in love, or feel attracted to a person, have a friendship, you can also be getting to know someone, another of them can be, wedding date, birthday, when you travel to see a person to your country, the excitement of being expecting a child, finish a career, and the list goes on, there are many kinds of emotions. Let's define emotions for being in love, they are transient, as they can also be permanent. The fleeting ones are when you do not know the person well, but they make you happy at that moment, and at the same time it is because you are thinking about something permanent, in fact it is what we all look for.

Emotions can be very confusing, we believe they are true, and everything we are going through and living in that moment, we do not think about the consequences, which in some cases can be fatal or destructive. Many of us, we travel to another country, hours, and hours of flight, all happy because we are going to see or meet someone, but the first impression is not what you expect. But when two or three days go by, the caresses, kisses, and everything else arrive, and we get a negative impression.

Sometimes it happens, that the male person does not have erections. For any woman in this case, all the emotions, energy, patience, time, and traveling far away, all those emotions go down. Because after being with that person and believing themselves to be happy, at that moment everything changes. Then they think they must start all over again and try to get rid of the frustration or be reborn again. No woman is going to have a partner who cannot make her sexually happy, and that is the beginning of a formal or permanent relationship. We are talking about human feelings, which are complicated and difficult to understand. Day by day we must deal with them, no matter how difficult they are, either with your boyfriend, husband, your children, family, or friends, but above all with the human beings that surround you daily. Let's remember, we must have our own personality. Living in the world and in our world, we must be aware that we all think differently, concentrate, and so on, we allow every situation and feeling to be slightly, unintentionally, accommodated. Which is important to know what you want in life, to learn to control your emotions or they will control you… even in your best moments.

The world we live in

In the world in which we live we can witness wrongful convictions for crimes not committed, unfortunately the facts of the truth never come to light. There are also many arguments where the injustices themselves drive you to suicide, because when you are doing time in jail it could be that one of your family members may not get a chance to see you for the last time. Many of them don't see the meaning of life and don't want to go on living; they don't understand so much injustice. I was observing a case, a lady whose son had been killed while she was in jail, she was devastated, she had no peace, she did not see the meaning of life, but what I could notice was that she was still listening to the word of our Lord Jesus Christ, and one as a human being would like to find the right word; so that they can find peace and tranquility, but unfortunately it is not so, it is something that only the one who is living it can really understand that pain, as is the feelings of loss, where sometimes the helplessness does not let you find an immediate solution. Only time can close the deep wounds.

Wounds that not even doctors can heal; only the Lord Jesus Christ is speaking to us little by little, and in the course, we can see the difference, also look at the circumstantial world, where we see that there are other people whose problems are greater. And as they say the worst thing is death, but sooner or later, we will reach that point, we just do not want to live it before our children. But only God has that answer. There are many secrets in life, and one as a human being with many deep feelings, that we will never get to understand everything, there are always some small ones and some big ones, and somehow, we must be strong to endure them. When we see some similar stories, to be there to support and bear with them what in some way or another we are going to live. That is the immediate consolation in which our soul perceives. Many times, we let ourselves be influenced and end up paying for other people's broken dishes.

Interpretation:
Each one of us was born with our own personality, some of us have more than one; and to control each one of them is not easy. If we try to be ourselves, life becomes easier, and we avoid so many of the problems we face daily. For those who think they are strong and handsome, think that everything passes them by, those are the most vulnerable and weak, those who always have something to worry about, and live their life in turmoil.

Observation:
Everything is easier when you think a little bit before you act; try to find the evil instincts, act intelligently, and you'll discover that from one minute to the next you can accomplish many things. As well as from one minute to the next you can lose a lot.

Prayer: Lord Jesus Christ help me with my insecurities, I want to be a worthy human being and compatible to understand other human beings.

In this world, no one has been able to adapt to the reality of the truths in which we live, and the truth is that we do not put our feet on the ground and understand that we are human beings with limited life, if we talk about putting our feet on the ground does not mean that all the time we will think about the future, or that at 60 years old we will be old, and that our life is over. But that does not mean that we should live a rushed life or try to make the most of it because time is running out. That is where we start to make mistakes and want to gain time. Sometimes we want to retire early to rest at home and go on vacation. We are offered businesses in which we are going to earn part of a good money to retire, but sometimes things don't work out, because some businesses are not legal, and we end up behind bars. If you are going to live 80 years you are only going to enjoy 70; in the world we live in, we are the ones who make the decisions and how long our life can be. It depends on our actions. It doesn't matter how long you live what matters is that you know how to live. Many of us, when we desire any purpose and we achieve it, we feel fulfilled and happy, that means that the purpose may be small, but I can bring a smile on our face, that's what really matters. And compared to all the material things, which most of us think make us happy, and to tell you the truth they do make you happy for a moment. But sometimes we have the things, and we don't appreciate them.

Interpretation:

Somehow, we all know it's like that, but we don't assimilate it correctly. And even though we lived it every day, with everything that happens in the world, sometimes we don't believe it, just because we are not there at the time of the events. We just see it and we are amazed, but at the same time we forget it. By this we do not mean that we are going to think about the tragedy all the time.

What we want is for there to be a change in our lives, to be a better person, humble, to understand that we are not made of iron, we are made of flesh and bones, and very fragile; so much so that no matter our age, stature, color or size, we can cease to exist from one minute to the next; all the survivors of this world that we have seen, only the soul and spirit can be saved and rescued from so much tragedy. We have witnessed the catastrophic tsunamis where it sweeps away everything it reaches, all the earthquakes in different countries, the rainstorms, sweeping mud and volcanic lava, moving houses and people as if they were garbage. We have seen all the car crashes, with all the occupants dead, planes crashing leaving only the pieces, human beings destroying one another, with guns, shooting each other to death. Among many other diseases in which you have little time to live. In this world it is not about judging or deciding the life of another. The world is the world. And we cannot change it, what we can do is to improve it. It is up to us to make the world different. Look at the examples of children who are often born with illnesses and defects, we have all seen how they have tried to survive in hospitals and somehow bring a smile to their parents. Many of them manage to recover and are exemplary in the future of other children. We must be aware of the world we live in and be a mirror for others.

Confinement

Confinement is a word that scares anyone. But some people like it and get used to it; we live in a very distant and scandalous environment, and as they say, even beauty is tiring. Enclosure is often mental, because sometimes we can go out everywhere and we prefer to stay at home, or we have the chance to have fun and decide to do family activities. In this opportunity I am going to tell a very special case, this lady called Maria, she had to be locked up in her grandmother's house. She had different personalities, sometimes she was angry and other times she was super happy. Because of her craziness she limped as she walked from side to side, back and forth, almost for the whole day. Maria was about 50 years old, but with incredible energy.

She loved to sing, dance, she looked like a celebrity. She just lived in her own mental world, so people didn't pay attention to her. But I paid a lot of attention to her, the songs she sang, they were spectacular, they seemed as if she had been a singer once. Her spirit was like that of a 15-year-old girl. There came a time when her family could no longer care for her. They had to send her to a camp where there were more than 1,500 women locked up for different reasons.

Maria was the only one who showed tranquility, she enjoyed her time, of course, wrapped up in her mental confinement. She could not assimilate whether she was locked up or outside. She said she was walking the streets of New York and with her laughter and stories she made other people laugh, quite a character. In conclusion, as we mentioned before, sometimes confinement is mental, and we must learn to laugh with it, because in many cases we can end up in psychiatry, taking a lot of medication. This would really cause us to be locked up forever.

Secret enemies

When we talk about an enemy it can be anyone who is around you and sometimes it can be closer to you than you imagine. They are very difficult enemies to detect. It is possible that it could be someone you know. They disguise themselves with the attitude of a friend, and act with many precautions to confuse you. Even if it is one of the people you know, it is difficult for you to suspect them. They are practically invisible, and you may be able to discover them if someone else comes along and removes their mask, because they have already done similar things to that same person.

Scene:
A woman who disguised herself as a church woman and claimed to be sent by God to help human beings with testimonies, but she was disguised, she was a demon in a human body. She had that opportunity because she lived in an institution, in a small community where everyone affected was in one problem or another. They felt they were at a dead end. They all approached the lady for help. Many of them had deportation problems. For her, they were the most important victims since she asked them for personal information to use when they were not in the country. The lady used their credit lines to live a crazy rich life at the expense of others. Since this person could no longer use her documents, it was very difficult to discover her, because no one was monitoring the system.

Indications:
Don't take a chance with anyone if you don't know them. There are many unscrupulous strangers who disguise themselves as saints and say they are sent by God. They convince others that they are super gifted and even if you

have a need, ask God for it yourself, use your faith and ask with your own mouth. Speak of your needs, and you will notice the difference. You don't have to ask someone else just like you. It is better to have direct contact because God knows your needs. Sometimes when you want to fix your problem, everything becomes a drama. When you have no proof to accuse directly sometimes it is better to forget everything and start over. When it comes to getting to know another person, we must have our limitations, not to give them too much confidence and our identity; that is your whole life.

In many of the cases, they use your identity and commit a homicide, it turns out that they find your identity at the place of the crime. They are going to investigate you and punish you until proven otherwise. Then your life becomes hell and so does your family's. You must have that instinct to be wary of strangers and think carefully before you decide or speak. Things that belong only to you mean victory, think of our past experiences and from a bad experience make a good thing, and what we have farthest away is what is closest to us. These are the possible intensities that one as a human being is exposed to.

Hope

In this world we all live on hope, that is what keeps us alive and with our souls high. Sometimes we have mixed feelings, when we rest in the hope that one day, we can achieve that, which keeps us strong. Fight and stand up, because among so much pain sometimes we lose even the strength of our thoughts, which are blocked to the point that many of us end up in total madness. When we take refuge in anything positive, we already think we are going to get what we want, and when it is not possible for us in the way we want, we give up and refuse to continue our daily struggle. It is important to always keep in mind that when we have high expectations and we get them at the planned time, it can also be that we do not get them the way we want them. Our expectations fall to the ground, then the mental depression begins.

For that reason, we cannot let ourselves be carried away by the quick moment. Keep in mind that good things take time. We all know that what comes fast, goes fast, with the difference that when you wait patiently you get what you waited so long for. You will value it more and take care of it more above all things. We must consider that hope is ourselves, without counting on friends, families or false offers or promises. Many of us believe in them as if they were real things. Things that the only thing they do is make us waste our time, because they are never going to reach our hands.

Observation:
Sometimes when we have been deceived for a lifetime, we think that our friends and our family members are with us. We hope that in any time of need you will be able to count on them. And you get the surprise that

even though they are your own family, you can't count on them, even for the smallest thing; they only criticize what really has value and the things they can't do, and the moment comes when you must make decisions, because your life can't go on with hypocrisy seeing how other human beings act and how they laugh in your face. Sometimes, even if we are dying inside, we will try to hide it just to not make them feel bad.

What a shame and what a pain to see how someone can have so much cynicism when you have given your best, and in the end, you end up disappointed. There was a girl named Carmencita, who went through a lot of foolish things. The only thing is that she didn't notice it, since she never asked for help, she always did things on her own. Carmencita did not like to ask for help. In her mind she understood that everyone had their own problems. She tried to do her things with a lot of effort, but she didn't judge anyone either; for the same reason, there is always a moment where you are going to need someone.

Then you have no choice but to ask for help, even if it's against your will. That's the way it is, we are human beings, and we need each other. That's why in this world we have doctors, priests, and a lot of community help. And even though we want to be alone or do things alone it is impossible. Because even animals share together. Birds fly together, I think we already know that when birds fly and if one bird's wings fail, one goes under the injured bird for support. In Carmencita's case, she said she needed family support. She was at a dead end. Unfortunately, she could not see what she expected; in moments like these the only thing that awaits you is to have hope from those people who have the possibility to do something when you need it the most. And that is when you realize that you are more alone than you thought, and even if you had hope at that moment, you feel that once again everything is falling to the ground. With many cries and sadness, you look up and down without knowing what to do. But you still have hope in God, and you ask him because he is the only one who will answer sooner or later. In the end those people who weren't there for you in those difficult times will regret it. And when it is their turn to suffer, they will need help. With the only difference that as all people are not equal, Carmencita showed them that in this life nothing is nothing, to understand that we cannot be someone when we are not someone with our own and even those who are not our own. As we say, today for you and tomorrow for me.

I am here but I am not being myself

The theme of, I am here, but I am not being myself: it is something that all human beings go through, but many do not really understand what it means, sometimes you find yourself in a place and what you are living is very far from who you really are. You don't really believe what is happening.

You say to yourself, I'm here but it's not me: the sad part of the situation is that you really are in that place, you just can't assimilate it, and the atrocities you are going through; example: you always tried to do your things right, to make everyone proud of you. Your children, your parents, your siblings, and friends. The blows of life lead you to do different things, that maybe all the good things you did, collapse at that moment.

You never imagined being in jail and living a hell in your own flesh, where the people you share your life with, take out their claws and attack you from behind, and where you also become the person, you are not, to defend your skin. Have you ever decided to share your life with someone, thinking you knew them... and then you discover that you are sleeping with a murderer, rapist, thief, and manipulator. As well as sharing and living with people who are alive by chance, because since their upbringing they lived terrifying childhoods. Practically they are only alive to tell the opposite, because their mind and personality are not what they would like or could be, due to the fact of being raped since they were 5 years old by their own parents or close relatives, but they are also used to witness sexual acts with other couples. Where just being there and listening, the only thing you can say is: I'M HERE BUT IT'S NOT ME.

Sure, it sounds ironic, it's easy to say it, the hard part is living it. In turn, being there and being you who is living the things that are happening around, being able to feel them with joy not with pain, because when you feel it, you are a totally different person than the one you really are, for having gone through those moments that do not allow you to enjoy the place or be with the right person.

On the other hand, it is difficult to say or avoid such situations, since many times they are surprises that you never expect in the world we live in. It is important to keep our eyes open for anything strange, or rather when something does not agree with us as human beings, we must act if we fit in a conversation or on a date, nightclub etc., Being in a place and feel that you are not you, at that moment you can have consequences.

For some reason you may put a lot of trust in the people around you, and the surprise may be permanent. With intelligence so that our feelings do not get destroyed, or diminished to a disturbing mental level where on many occasions we survive with pills to fight depression because of all that we have lived through. If you do not feel as normal, that is why I wrote this topic, so that each of us can look in the mirror and deduce the high and low of our life's day by day.

Experience

From the time you are born until you die everything is experiences and more experiences, your first steps, your first word, and from 10 to 20 years old, a stage in which you think a lot about beauty, many think about going to school, and it is possible that we have some ideas for when we finish our studies, and if you want to go to college or how many suitors or boyfriends you have. Everything is an experience, you enjoy them all, most of the time they are made easy, due to still having the support of your parents, if you keep going to college and you have their convenience and support, and if not, you must do it with your own effort.

There, you start your own job search experience, and at the same time, being good at what you do, because if you do not, they'll fire you and look for someone else instead of you, your experience means that you must be better at all the things you aim to do in your daily life. Experiences can leave cut marks that are difficult to heal. That is why they are experiences, to learn from them and not let them happen again. But these are things that cannot be predicted, they happen during our daily life; and from the good or bad things we do, therefore we must keep our eyes wide open so that the experience to come, will not surprise us, but rather we should try to surprise it. That is, to act intelligently and to not take surprises that can end our lives. I believe that being born and living is the most beautiful experience a human being can have; it is the experience that makes us grow in every way. As we live a different quality of life, it makes us laugh at what we used to experience before. That doesn't mean that we should go through bad lives, we should first try to lead our life in a positive way rather than going through bad moments. We were born to be happy, and we are responsible for what we do. We should try to live and die in harmony.

Happiness

Happiness is a very large and highly expected topic. We all think that happiness is being rich, but we are totally wrong. Being rich covers a part of your happiness, and that's when you realize that you lack other things. Sometimes you feel empty, and you look around you and feel that, even though you have everything, you are missing something. In my case I was able to discover that what made me happy was to achieve the projects and goals I had, and to be close to my family. On the other hand, being happy with my husband even though we were not rich, but the most important thing is to get along well and work together for a purpose and achieve the necessary things in life. That's what leads you to happiness all the time.

As human beings we need to think, one of the things that leads to the other, if they are well thought out, analyzed, and shared with the people we love. Many of us think that having material things will make us happy, but unfortunately it is not so, because you are happy for a moment, and then come difficult periods that we do not know how to handle. We will also find many days in which we will long have other things that will truly make us happy. Happiness does not need to be material. There are many ways to be happy, but we must discover what really makes us happy. We are all different. The message is that priorities must be performed to complete the intensity and feelings of us, human beings.

The Ugly

No one wants to hear the word ugly, since it is not only about human beings, but also about objects such as cars, furniture, houses, clothes, etc. So, we think that what is ugly has no value, nor can it be seen normally; that is what many think is so, and unfortunately it lowers their self-esteem, and they get to the point of falling into depression completely, and do not want to hear or spend time with anyone. But that should not be so, and we all know that.

Nowadays there are so many wonders; it is not because of plastic surgeons, but it is how you want to change your personality, no matter if people call you ugly, for example sometimes we want to have thin noses and many times it does not go with our personality. Many people have wide or broad noses and look spectacular, as well as full or thin lips; and at the end of the day, it doesn't make a difference. It is about our self-confidence or, at the very least, feeling or becoming comfortable with ourselves.

We refer to the way we speak; how you laugh, how your teeth are; when it comes to your hair, we know you can wear wigs, extensions; and with your body, a good diet, and a lot of exercise, you can achieve whatever you set your mind to.

These are tips that we all know, but sometimes we don't practice them. Actually, let's get to the point, what is involved in being ugly, there is no one ugly, if we at least know how to dress up, although admittedly there are some that are quite unattractive, and in fact are super ugly, to the point that women become men or take hormones to look more masculine. As a woman it is impossible to see how men are beautiful because there is nothing to criticize. Let's remember that everyone has their own sex ap-peal (sexual attraction) to conquer what they want. Do not forget the things you want, on the contrary, what you achieve in life is what will make you show the beauty that you may not have, and accompanied by a lot of sympathy, but above all have a lot of self-confidence.

To be convincing and not to fail oneself we must avoid that, because if you do it yourself; then what will others say, that's what we must avoid, that's what gives us the opportunity to have our own personality and beauty regardless of anything else. T

his topic is directed to all those who are afraid and insecure, of being or becoming. We are not saying that it is easy, for the same reason, we must motivate ourselves to write and help a little in what we already know, especially that it is not too much to add all the benefits and challenges in our life, because that implies our happiness, but above all to couple our feelings, which always haunt us. Without counting our enemies who are always with notes and accusations.

Frustration

When I was nine years old, my frustration began. I lived from house to house trying to work so they would let me study, since I wanted to improve myself; I knew that life was difficult. At that age many took advantage of me, not only did I have to take care of children younger than me, but I also had to clean the whole house. Sometimes I couldn't keep up with schoolwork. When I got out of school, I had to cook, take care of the children and everything else. Then there came a time when the house where I was staying told me about another job, like what I was already doing, with the difference that the lady of the house helped a little, but I felt like a prisoner because I could not go anywhere.

Eventually I contacted my family who lived about three hours away from where I was living. Then I decided to return, but not to my parents' house, but to another house where I had to pay rent. At that time, I was already 14 years old, I decided to look for a job and thank God, I found it. It was a little different because I could study and work at the same time. During my 14 to 17 years, it was a nightmare. I was studying at night, walking down the street to my house. One night someone came by and said he would take me home. I was already tired of walking. I decided to ride with him, but the fatal thing was that he didn't take me home, he wanted to rape me, fortunately I managed to escape and kept running. I was very desperate; it was night, and I didn't know what to do at that moment. Time passed and when I thought my life was going to change, another stage began. My first pregnancy with a man who turned out to be very bad. When I went to sleep, I would lie down on the bed, he would remove the top mattress until I was thrown on the floor. From that moment on I hated him terribly, and at the same time I couldn't leave the house, because I had nowhere to go. So, I had to stay there and put up with all the abuse. It was not a happy pregnancy; after 4 years I got pregnant again; it was even worse. At that time, I was more prepared to leave home because I also had a job to pay for all my things. I felt such a great hatred for him that I didn't even want to see him. He wouldn't stop bothering me, he wouldn't leave me alone. He always chased me and made me fight with him a lot at my workplace. My life became desperate, apart from the fact that he chased me, broke the windows of the cars and the windows of the house, and stole all my savings. He would do it carefully to avoid leaving traces. He would also come to the window of my house to wait for me at night, until I managed to get a restraining order against him. So, I was able to push him away for a little bit, but he didn't really care. After all this, I could be calm for a while and decided to stay alone to raise my children. And so, the years went by, many suitors approached me, but they were not worth it. Many of them wanted to take the little I had.

They didn't even want to work, some of them were vicious, so I felt very frustrated to the point that I didn't want to have anyone. Then I decided to take a vacation with my children and travel to my country. There I met a young man who, by the way, we had studied together in school. Since there was already a little trust between the two of us, we decided to start a small business selling clothes and other merchandise. He took over because I could not stay in my country. I trusted him a lot, but it turned out to be a disaster. He ran the business into the ground, sold all the merchandise and took all the money. I never saw him again, but I forgot about it, I never asked him to pay me back. Again, time passed, and I met another boy, he was not really my prince charming, but he had many qualities that caught my attention. He was honest, attentive, compatible, and familiar. During that time, we got to know each other better and started a relationship. Then something unexpected happened where I had to move to another country for a while due to family problems. I trusted him to take care of the house, since I had no other option and no one else. After two or three months, he was not taking care of anything in the house. Just because I wasn't there, his mind didn't work the same, and then everything fell apart. I was worried about what I was going to have to face when I got back; I was going to have nowhere to live. It was very frustrating for me, I felt like I was between a rock and a hard place with nothing I could do. Sometimes I called on the phone hoping to hear a word of encouragement and I only heard bad news, I was afraid to call, but I was so anxious about not hearing from my children every time I tried to contact them.

Interpretation:
It is sad to spend your life expecting good things, only to receive blows and disappointments. Now my mind only thinks of all those ugly things, that I wouldn't wish even to my worst enemy. Sometimes I pretended to not think or cry, but even if you don't want to, you get frustrated. You don't think about anything positive. You don't believe in anything anymore; it's hard after trying to get some happiness and not having good results.

Life expectancy:
In all these sufferings, God never stopped loving me, and accompanying me in those difficult moments. My God always spoke to me with words of encouragement, giving me strength to continue with my life, where I still had a long way to go. There was a moment when God told me: *Do not worry about yesterday's pain, and let the rain wash away today's pain. All of them will honor you with all blessings and many of them will come to you with their sorrowful souls asking for forgiveness.*

Thank you, God, for the life you gave me

It is said from the moment we are in our mother's womb our lives have come with a destiny. But the truth is that we should thank God for the mere fact of coming into the world and for having the pleasure of enjoying the wonders of the universe. From the time you are a baby, grow up and become a teenager until you become an adult, there are different stages. Then we can know what we want and choose what we want in our lives. If you are born with a talent, it is a game changer in your life because it is something you develop to be a successful person and feel proud and admired by many.

Others are not born with the same luck, but we should not deny that we were born, no matter how good or bad it may be. We are human beings who bring life, therefore, productive beings. It is possible that you were not what you wanted to be in life, but your children can be successful people and you can see yourself in the mirror of your children, because sometimes when we deny the luck we have, things become more difficult for us.

It is important to keep calm and not to despair, but above all to consider that what makes one unhappy, makes another happy. We are a world, and we have the option or the decision to do it in many ways, in which we can feel comfortable, happy, and not worried because life is only one.

Ignorance

The ignorance of human beings, for anyone who identifies with it. In life many believe that by sitting in front of a computer they are already professionals or entrepreneurs, knowing that they never went to college, but that does not mean anything, since many do not go to college and behave as such. Thus, respecting employees, family and friends, and act as if they were better than others, when deep down they are nothing.

In many of the cases they believe their own lies, to the point that they drown in their own deep waters. For those who are not ignorant, it is easy to understand. Sometimes there are people who, although they have something, it is as if they have nothing. Because they feel empty inside. What a pity, because they are people who lived with dysfunctional families and never got over it, to the point that they enjoy seeing others suffer and participate in them without thinking about the future consequences. Ignorance does not allow us to see the mistakes we make in life. Not forgetting that our Lord Jesus Christ was judged and sacrificed, he was also killed. It is important to remember that everything will fall by its own weight, and sometimes, even if you are standing, you will feel as if you were lying down.

How nice to be able to write a topic where everyone can scrutinize a bit. In the month of November Thanksgiving, giving thanks to God and to all those who did their best to put their two cents to help those in need, thus becoming heroes to God's eyes. At the end of the day that is all we take with us in life.

Impotence

What it feels like when you are impotent, wanting to do something and not being able to do it. In this topic we talk about the helplessness of confinement, where you could not leave, and you were only given news that is difficult to endure. There comes a time when you feel you want to leave and fly to a place where you are needed; impotence is not enough because it is something stronger than you, and that you cannot control: What is impotence for you? It can be categorized in different positions; for example, how important is what you left behind, and because of circumstances you can't do anything.

Sometimes you feel that your nervous system can be your worst enemy; where you don't eat, or when you use the bathroom and can't relieve yourself, and even though you are sitting, your feet won't stop shaking, you cry non-stop, and your stomach runs from side to side causing uncontrollable diarrhea and, in many cases, suicide attempts. This is a true story of Mrs. Vanessa, where her helplessness was that she was given 25 years in prison. During her time of incarceration, she went through much suffering, until she became somewhat accustomed to her other cellmates. Her family rarely visited her.

In her mind she would always keep hoping because there was someone very special, he was her son, her adoration, her only son, he kept her going, with the hope of being able to be with him again, someday and in the course of that time her family received news and they didn't know how to notify her that her son had been shot in the head in a barbershop in New York. For the family and friends, the helplessness was immeasurable, it was as if they had also killed her, for not being able to see her first born, and not being able to be there in his last days, because the authorities did not let her go out to see him. We consider this type of news to be number one, although we should know that all human beings are different. Some of us are stronger and others are weaker. In the case of Mrs. Vanessa, she never resigned herself, and that is where the impotence takes over you and you feel helpless, and it traps you.

When you feel that you lose everything, I am not referring to material things, it is when you lose your dignity, your pleasures, your freedom, your friendships, and above all to make your own decisions. That is when we start to think about the meaning of impotence, where reality is reality, as for example: a woman had a daughter who got her period at an early age and became pregnant at the age of 9. These are surprises and realities that become impotence, as we already know you can't do anything, you only have worries and you feel trapped; another example of impotence is when you have been attacked by your enemies, the reaction we have as human beings, is to attack them too in defense, no matter what happens, if you come out alive or you come out dead.

Scene:
This was a boy named William, it was a rainy night, he had gone out to play dominoes with his friends, they were betting money. One of the friends had lost, so he lost control and decided to take a machete and wanted to kill William, he only managed to cut him in the right eye, he got desperate and was able to run away. But not only to run away, it was to look for another machete to kill his adversary. And when he arrived at the house, my mother and I saw him bleeding with the machete in his hand, we were able to grab him to avoid a bigger tragedy, because from there anyone could get killed, then my mother and I managed to keep him from coming

back, he didn't want to stay with the wound and not being able to do anything; the helplessness at that moment was unbearable, but my mother and I were able to overcome the impotence of seeing how a family member suffered. In all this the most important thing was to be able to prevent a small tragedy from becoming bigger, because from something so small it could turn into something frightening, they could kill each other and go to jail.

Messages:

If only we could all avoid all these sorrows, and that in every negative situation that comes our way, there would be less suffering.

Decisions and questions
Which do you prefer, to be alive or dead?

Which do you prefer, to be blind or to see?

Which do you prefer, to be imprisoned or free?

Which do you prefer, to walk straight or to walk lame, or to be in a wheelchair?

Which do you prefer, to have friends or to be alone?

What do you prefer, to be a professional or to have any type of self-development, or to be one of those who spend their life begging?

What do you prefer, to have a healthy life or to live sick, or to go through different opinions or rushed decisions?

What is the point of all these questions?

Observation:

We must ask ourselves day by day; how can we avoid all these things that bring us these problems? It is difficult to predict, since they are surprises that life gives us without us expecting them. If we act intelligently, we can avoid many of them, and look for real motivations, where our feelings take us to the place where we all want to be.

Interpretation:

When we talk about observations, they are small ideas that we can use in reference in our daily life. We should interpret all these crossroads that all human beings must go through, and many times they are difficult to control, or predict. We must be prepared little by little for when they come to us. In this world we are exposed to everything, and always. We as adults must lead our children to grow up with good feelings to prevent them from being gang members, hitmen, thieves, drug addicts; but above all, we must not let them act on instinct. In these times that a child may not be treated as a child.

We adults, day by day, must be firm and strong because there are many moments in which we let ourselves be influenced by the filth of the world. Rather, we must focus on mental and physical health. This helps us to become real and different people in the stages of our lives. If we follow these tips, we human beings can make a difference, bringing to others a positive message that we all need.

My disability won't stop me

Narrative by Jennie Aldrich

There are billions of people on earth and more than a handful of them, have a disability. There are so many disabilities in this world ranging from mild to severe. Some are visible and some are not, affecting an individual's way of thinking and/or movement. Some people are disabled to the point that they need to be in a wheelchair and others who live completely independent live with little help from others. For example, I have Cerebral Palsy, which is a physical disability that affects the signal in my brain, that controls my body movements, including my speech. I have suffered mental health problems because I feel useless due to my disability. I did not accept that I had a condition and was angry that I did not have a normal life. When my mental illness was under control, I went to college, went to a few different programs to make my life more valuable and I keep busy reading, doing crafts, going to the gym a few days a week.

Even though I have difficult days when I am in physical pain, I know I get through it as I have in the past. Because I understand some people have it worse than me. Aside from my disability, there are many other types in which a person can be disabled. Autism is an example of a disability that is more affected by the mind. There are also different levels of this disability. One factor of autism is that an individual's social skills are very low. They have difficulty in social situations and because of that they have trouble establishing or maintaining relationships with people outside of their family. There is also a level of autism where an individual cannot speak, therefore, they need a communication device or a caregiver who is trained to help them. Some of these aspects of this disability can also be found in Down syndrome. There are so many other disabilities that a person can have. Some people may even have more than one.

No matter what a person's disability is, strive to have the best life possible. Many people who are disabled join special Olympics to be active and make friends. I spent many years competing in swimming and skiing and made good relationships with others. There are also day programs that people can attend to have a more fulfilling life. In the end we are human beings, we should feel as happy and loved by everyone else.

End of Jennie Aldrich's narrative.

Going away

All human beings at one time or another need a vacation. It may be that we don't go on a cruise or a day at the beach. That doesn't mean getting away from problems, but getting away from everything that is suffocating you, at that instance. Sometimes you feel that you are living in toxic moments, and you feel that you are going to go crazy, that you want to explode. Sometimes what we did with our hands we undo with our feet. That happens when your body can't take it anymore. And the worst thing is that you end up regretting that moment of rage that you could not control.

Example:
When I was living in my hometown I was going through many processes, they were accumulating residues of many rages for different decisions that I was facing day by day. They accumulated for 16 years, I felt very depressed. I didn't feel like living, I didn't see any sense in my life. Everything around me seemed to be fine, but all my sadness could be seen on my face to the point that I could not concentrate on anything I was doing. But there was something that hurt me, and it was always on my mind.

It was that for all those years, I had been the hero in that I wanted everything to be perfect, and that no one would hold petty things against me. My pride was that if I touched something I wanted to move it too. But I also liked to share everything I did to make me proud and to make others proud. But inside me, I felt this deep emptiness, that no matter what I did at that moment, it was as if my personality didn't exist, and there was someone telling me that I was perfect. I wanted and needed to bring my body back to life, since I didn't seem to care about anything around me. It was then that I made the decision to move away to another state and get away from everything that was vitiating me, to fill all the emptiness I felt inside me, fortunately I was able to do it little by little.

I was able to find myself again and think about what really made me happy and satisfied me as a woman, mother, or daughter. I learned to value even the smallest things that I didn't give importance to before. Sometimes we believe that our bodies are machines, that they work with fuel, but no, it is not so! We are human beings with feelings that need our space to think and analyze all the negative things, and make sure that they do not become nightmares that prevent us and others from being happy. And when you reunite with yourself you already come back with a different life, ready to continue with a new life.

Observation:
Going far away includes mental exercises, such as yoga, walking, listening to music, dancing, and above all communication with our Lord Jesus Christ. It is important to ask our father to help us with the life change we want, and if we ask with faith, we can be sure that we will receive all our requests.

Youth

Youth is the most beautiful thing we have when we begin to live. Youth does not mean when we are young, even if you are as old as you are. And even if you feel young inside and you consider that you have energy, that can be called permanent youth, we all know that when you keep your body exercised and you don't have bad habits you can always be young. The difficult thing is to follow the rules, for some people it is very difficult, there are ways to motivate yourself, one of them is if you are in love and you want your partner to see you beautiful, if you are 20 years old and you see a woman of 40 with a spectacular body, that gives you hope.

Anyway, there are many, but especially if you stay healthy, apart from everything we have talked about, during our youth we can be complicated, since many of us use it for good and others use it for bad. I mean when you are young to study and be a better person in life. That is, to create your own striking personality, because you can be young but not pretty. Sometimes you can be an ugly person and you show a good personality, that makes you the most beautiful person. Sometimes you can be an ugly person and have a great personality, that makes you the most beautiful person. Put it into practice and you will see how much you will achieve.

You must take advantage of your youth years, because as time goes by, you can no longer turn the clock back, and have the satisfaction of being with your partner, raising your children and accomplishing your goals. If you think about those things, even if you are in your middle age, and you reflect on all that you have lived, it will bring you great happiness. And even if you are sad, at that moment you will be happy, because of the things you lived in your youth and that made you happy. You will always carry that happiness in your heart. The intensity of youth is to keep the spirit alive, to give light to those around you and let them give life to you, and even if the years go by you will always be a young person.

Ambition and money

Money and ambition are two apparently equal things, two joint words. When we have ambition, we end up doing whatever it takes to get what we want. We all know that ambition is part of failure. You can become envious of your friends' things and become an unscrupulous person. In many cases it can be small or big, it all depends on how much you want to have, the more you want the higher the price you will pay.

Having ambition does not only mean having money or envy the things of others, but it may also be that you want to excel in life, such as being a doctor, lawyer, engineer etc. Just like any other career, but unfortunately, not all of us think beautifully of wanting to excel. The difficult thing is to finish, because sometimes we have reasons, such as lack of money and lack of intelligence. We must consider that, even if you cannot be a doctor or anything else in life, we can choose other options to have a healthy and uncomplicated life.

Because of our ambition for money, we make many mistakes because we always want to have more and more, which by the way has nothing wrong with it, but you must get it in a good way, with work, sacrifice and so you can enjoy it more. We all live confused, when we are close to anyone who has everything, living a comfortable life, we all want to be like that. Many people have everything, but they are not happy and suffer inside. They are in pieces and that leads them to make different decisions in life. It is almost impossible to say anything to someone who does not take advice. They like to go through those difficult processes and then they realize for themselves, that's when they understand that it's not all luxuries, cars, and everything else. When we talk about having ambition ... we don't measure the consequences, and we do even the most dangerous things, whatever it takes. Many carry drugs in their stomachs with the chance of dying on the way. In other words, to have money and to satisfy their ambition, they do not think about their lives and those of their families. Others end up in jail for many years, and many decide to steal.

Consequences:
We must understand that putting drugs in a human being or a child's stomach, in the end it becomes an atrocity, just to have a little money, and what is worse, keep committing that illegal action. Money is not going to last you a lifetime, yet we do it repeatedly until you get caught. You're not going to care how much you have or how much you made, and even if you have it, you're not going to enjoy it. Once you are locked up for 10 or 20 years in prison, you could become a millionaire, but those millions end up being enjoyed by others. Unfortunately, we realize situations like that, when we are living them, in a way that one can barely believe:

Scene:
When you have everything, there comes a time when you are left with nothing. Instead, you must ask or wait for your family to send you money. Just to see yourself in a prison wearing one color of clothes, going hungry, and waiting in line to be able to talk on the phone, in other words, you must wait to survive in that place. Another important thing, you lose your family and children, and that's when we say: "if I could start over, I would live a simple life with no money, I would settle for anything I could eat. In truth, anything would be better than what I am living, to live this life like a slave as in the old days, it's not worth it.

The cape and the power

The cape and the power are shells that cover the damaged parts, leaving on the surface all the good, but above all we must make clear that to form this cape we use the damaged parts purifying what is seen on the surface, so that nothing that could damage, or soil, could penetrate what is clean. With this shell, bullets slide off, fire won't burn your skin and falls won't hurt you. This is because the brightness of the garment makes all the negative things that have been accumulating for a long time to slide off.

When you are not covered with this cape you can visualize all the storms with the assurance that when evil wants to get close, there is very little damage it can do to you. The cape was designed for all who need it. And those who cannot acquire it still can have it. As we all know that to have something we have to struggle and be perseverant, I don't think it is so difficult, and those who consider that it is not easy to build that kind of cloak, then they have two options; either you make an effort so that you can form your shell or you will have to have the capacity so that when the storm comes to you, you will not fear it, you will not run away from it, and you will be strong enough to face everything that is coming....

Interpretation:

That shell that covers our human body is built by the courage of so many sufferings, relapses, illnesses, losses, and disappointments. It is a continuous struggle in which day by day it seems not to end. There were many human beings who felt that their heart was beating out of their chest, thinking that they were not going to resist, until they had to witness different scenes, while thinking that it was too much for one person, and if it had been one of them, they would have died in the attempt. This message persevered till the end and one of them was crawling in pain with their soul in pieces, but always fighting to the end. At least they were able to share in front of the whole world and be able to give a positive message saying that everyone can build their own garment and feel safe. Even if they were drowning, they can get afloat, and even if there is fire, they will not get burned, and if their heart is out of place, they can hold it with their hands.

Observation:

    With this cape you do not become invisible, it only teaches us that we must persevere, and become enduring, and exemplary human beings for those viewers with the same need.

The story of a boy named Carlos

He had everything and now, he had nothing

Since I was a child, I always had everything. My parents made sure that I lacked nothing, but as one always wants to be independent, I left home to do things on my own. The moment I wanted to start by myself, I realized that I didn't know how to do anything, and I was ashamed to go back to my parents' house, on the contrary, I wanted them to be proud of me and to show them that I could do it on my own. Of course, my parents wanted me to become a doctor or a professional so that I would not suffer in life, but I did not listen to them, and I did not do well. I had to decide, since I already had a wife and children to support, so I opted for the easiest option, and what we call easy is not easy, because the risk is too much.

There is the risk of being killed or kidnapped and at the same time of having your family members killed, as well as going to prison for many years, these are the things that one can hardly imagine. All you think about is the money you can earn without thinking about the reality of life, you may be killing little by little innocent people and apparently one does not see it that way, because they are of age, and sometimes we usually say: Whoever delights in dying, to them, death will taste like glory. It may be so, but the burden on your conscience will not let you live in peace. Also, you may live with one of their relatives, and that is when you really feel it. Then you become aware of everything you have done and secondly you also become more confident in the work you are doing. You don't take proper care of yourself before you know who's behind you and who's around you. I had everything and, in the end, I had nothing. I saved $300,000 in one year, all to myself and lost it all. I ended up in prison for 14 years. I didn't have my children or my wife, I said to myself, it's awful to feel empty, and to disappoint your parents and children, as well as losing your wife, and spending 14 years in prison, practically like being a slave. It is a slavery where every day, you must do what you must do.

Just imagining yourself doing the same thing for a whole week, you'll become almost insane. You should have a very good mind for it to work well. Throughout all these adversities, life is short as we already know and it is good to take advantage of it, with effort and sacrifice, and not to be at the mercy of other people who do not really care if you are happy or sad. They follow the laws with each one and even if you don't like it, it's up to you, not to choose what you really want to do.

This topic is dedicated for people who are blind to surprises. In life you make your own destiny. However, there is still time to change and not to be that way. Even if one does it for money, we all know that money helps a lot, but it is not everything, because as many of us know, when we have nothing, at least we will always get something to eat, and that is what they give you in prison, food, and on many occasions, you are not even able to eat it. I had a partner who also lost 2 million dollars, his houses and four cars, and every day we went to eat together. We couldn't even eat the food they gave us. He would cry and sometimes he couldn't believe what he was going through.

Conclusion:

Let us focus on our principles and think about the extent of our feelings for ourselves. Our family and all those we love, let's try to live a different life, to achieve different things, to feel with new life, without having to lose everything and to have a happy ending, not a dead ending, but a living ending.

We call her the coveted child

Because she was born with great virtues. They called her the human bible; she knew everything they asked her. The older people, loved to spend time with her and ask her difficult questions, just to hear the extraordinary things she talked about. And so, she grew up, studying, and with a lot of discipline. When the girl grew up, she was completely beautiful, everyone would be staring at her, because she had a spectacular body, when she went out for a walk in the neighborhood the car drivers stopped in front of her, just to talk to her, but she didn't care, she didn't buy it, and acted as if nothing happened.

The boys wanted to take her everywhere, restaurants, beaches, and parties. But what she loved to do most was to go to the mountains and ride motorcycles. She was always surrounded by many friends and received many gifts. When she was 16, her parents bought her first car. She learned to drive and went everywhere. She loved to serenade her friend's girlfriends in the neighborhood at night. She loved adventures, challenges, and going to exotic places.

There were places, where going up the streets was like climbing a three-hundred-meter tree. In that neighborhood, all the inhabitants were albinos, they had white eyelashes and white hair. Albinos are human beings with extraordinary and impressive characteristics, their skin colors are reddish, and the daughters of albinos are very beautiful. To be coveted is not only to be born rich or to have everything, but we must also emphasize that we always have that mentality. There are many children who come from a family that apparently has everything, but they do not feel happy. To be coveted is not necessarily to spend time with the person you love, we must remember that we cannot be carried away by what we have if we all must make sacrifices. Going to school, finishing a degree, and doing a lot of what some of her friends didn't get to do. Her friends were from very powerful families, many of them wanted to finish their careers.

In the case of the coveted girl, the whole neighborhood knew her, they were always looking for her for many activities, she was always willing, but she did not forget her goals and responsibilities. She used to always ready, but she did not forget her goals and responsibilities. She studied communications and she is now a businesswoman, she has a healthy life, she still spends time with some of her friends who by the way were never successful. If we notice, we complain about everything, nowadays, including the good things that happen to us. Even though, bad things will happen, we must try to make them seem good.

When you use this kind of strategies with yourself, life becomes easier... For example, if you live in a very boring place and you feel you have no life, create your own activities, such as traveling and seeing new places. Being coveted is mental, anyone can be coveted, and if you set your mind to it, you just must be positive with yourself, trust in your ability as a person without counting on someone else to help you. Just because you are young doesn't mean that they will think about you and your future all the time.

When you achieve goals and purposes you can say, I was a coveted girl but now I am a woman of challenges, goals, and fulfillment. You gain nothing by having it all, and although sometimes when you are small and have privileges, there are many who live with frustrations of having nothing and when they grow up, if they achieve those combinations, they will feel complete. You don't have to be waiting for other people to help you because we already know that they can do it once or twice, but by the third time they don't do it. Sometimes you are surprised, but life is like that... You yourself must have control over your feelings and not let others play with the most sacred thing that God could give us. Our pure and healthy feelings, which, because of life's mistakes, we spoil everything, losing ourselves in the horizon.

The long-suffering child

A little girl named Dulce was born in 1973. She was called the suffering child because many strange things happened to her in the camp where she lived. It was like a battlefield. There were packs of dogs with plague. Dulce had to hide in the drawers at the age of 5 because the dogs would be biting everyone, it was like a pandemic. Sometimes she had to hide for 4 or 5 days because all the dogs in the neighborhood where like a plague and no one could control them, even the older people had to hide. Her siblings would look for a place to hide, they would all be home alone, and their parents would be working.

As the hours passed, they managed to come out of hiding very hungry and with nothing to eat. Dulce had to go to other people's houses to get some food. There she would stay until her parents arrived home. When Dulce turned 10 years old, she was able to go to school, which by the way was very far away. It was almost a two-hour walk, but it was the closest school in the small town; but it was the closest school in the small town; anyhow, she had to study.

Thank God the girl had the desire to learn, she lasted two years in that school. Later, her parents decided to send her to the city with a niece, looking for a better future. Being in the city, everyone thought she was going to be better off, but unfortunately it was the opposite. The poor girl was only 12 years old and had to take care of 4 small children of the cousin where she lived. She had to do everything for those children; bathe them, feed them, and take care of them for the whole day. Dulce couldn't even go to school anymore. The purpose of taking Dulce to the city was not to help her but to take advantage of her. Dulce was also a child and liked to play and do other things like the other children. The cousin always went out with the children and Dulce had to stay at home. She would start crying with great sadness because she wanted to go out too, and they never wanted to take her. Dulce experienced panic attacks and she would start to crawl down the street. After a while they decided to enroll her in school in the afternoon. She had to get up at 5 a.m. to take care of the 4 children, cook and clean before she could go to school. Considering that the school was an hour away from where she lived.

Dulce did not get out of school until late at night and had to walk across very dangerous streets. On one of those nights a motorcycle came along and ran her over, knocking her unconscious. Some people decided to help her and took her to the nearest hospital, with the news that she had a broken leg and arm. After that, the relatives got scared and brought her back to the house with her mother. The excuse the cousin gave was that Dulce was misbehaving and they couldn't deal with her anymore.

Dulce's mother believed all the stories she was told and was furious. She took a metal bar and hit her on the head, until she drew blood. Little Dulce didn't know what to do anymore, she felt desperate and at a dead end. Everyone treated her badly, it was hopeless. By then Dulce was 15 years old, since she was a little older, her father took her to work, but it was very hard work.

They had to ride on horseback to the workplace. They would leave early in the morning and return at night. Dulce, with her little dark face as dirty as the soil. But all of that was not enough, Dulce had to carry water from a distant well to bathe. She felt tired, there were days when she didn't want to go to work with her father, her father would get upset and he would grab a cow's rope to reach her from a far distance, he would tie her legs leaving deep marks that looked like sores. Many times, those sores would get infected, and without the accessibility to any type of medications to treat them. And so, she still had to go to the river to wash clothes all day long.

The river was about an hour away from the house, up a mountain, a hill with wet clothes on her head. It was impossible for Dulce to think that there was any hope of being a happy person, or at least living a normal life like all girls her age. Until she decided to escape in search of new horizons, because her situation was unbearable; she wanted to start a new life again.

During this time Dulce met a friend and decided to look for a job in a family home. There, it was a little different because she was already making a little money and managed to survive; she was also able to study. That doesn't mean that the suffering stopped there, because in that house she was also treated badly, just because she was a maid. She had to hide when visitors arrived. For the patrons in those days, it was a sin to let oneself be seen being a maid. Those sufferings did not stop until Dulce was able to finish high school with additional courses to have a good job, so, she could avoid the mockery of everyone.

Dulce was interested in moving forward, so she could help her younger siblings and prevent them from going through the same thing. These were things she didn't wish on anyone. Dulce is now a woman. She did help her siblings, they were able to move to the city, and they were all able to go to school. Dulce is now a fulfilled person with her own children, and although she once was a suffering child, she could not forget her feelings for her parents and siblings. She managed to have her whole family with her and reduced the needs as much as possible. In fact, this is a living example of a suffering child who, if she had forgotten everyone and everything because of her suffering, she would not feel as she does now. Sometimes even though suffering is not easy to forget, especially when it comes from our parents. It is important to overcome those bad moments, and never forget the real family.

Because in one way or another, family is always going to be family. After a while she met her cousin, the mother of the four children she was taking care of, and she was surprised to find out that she had gone completely insane, so crazy that she would take off her clothes on the street while at the same time wanting to kill herself. This teaches us that no matter how good our life is, we should not forget where we come from and where we are going. Understand that God controls our destiny, in a secret way, and that when we do harm to our neighbor, we are doing it to ourselves.

The reality of life

Life is a reality, but we don't see it that way. When we are in trouble, we make up an excuse or a lie to make ourselves look good at the time, without realizing that this excuse or lie can lead us into a deep hole with no way out. Nor do we realize that a small lie becomes a big one. At that moment we are happy, because people believe everything, and things work out well for us. Then time goes by, and it turns out that the past meets the present and we see that many things do not match. As we are used to lie, we go from excuse to excuse, and we make the problem bigger.

Examples:
When you lie to your partner and it turns out that you are with someone else outside of the marriage, these are things you can't hide. Unfortunately, it is a bitter reality when you have a real marriage. That's when you realize you're going to have a lot of problems.

A son hides from his father all the bad things he is doing with his friends. When something hard to hide happens, the son has no choice but to come forward with the truth, because he needs his father's help.

Stealing money from your job just because you think you won't get caught. Many people find it easy, and they don't think that when they take inventory the owners of the company start to investigate, and they end up being caught. Then you understand the reality of life.

We human beings insist on living in lies. Those that lead us to suffer and then we end up destroying ourselves unconsciously. Then we start to complain saying that we have bad luck, next we think why these things have happened to us. We do not realize that we ourselves are the ones who destroy our lives.

There is a very important case that happened to a man named Pablo, 54 years old; his life was not real. Everything he spoke or said was a lie, when he said things there was no one who could believe him. He said it with so much nature that not even a psychologist could detect it; it was already a disease. He had the opportunity to be sincere and speak the truth, but he felt a satisfaction, when they believed him, for him it was a success.

For Pablo it was already normal, since he started with his lies when he was 10 years old. Everyone who knew him already knew who he was, but those who did not know him believed all his lies. Don't think that I am talking about any person who has nothing to lose. In the eyes of many, Pablo was a person of respect, a family man, and a police officer. So, he used all his attributes to make his lies look like reality.

To give you an idea of what this character could say, I will give you an example of one of his lies. Mr. Pablo said that every day he won money in the lottery. He said he had millions of dollars in the bank and that he came from a wealthy family, and that his relatives were already retired. That's what he told the girls he dated. In his mind he thought he could win them over; the girls believed it all because it seemed true.

They could not believe that a person with so much respect, could make up thousands of such absurd lies. One of the girls he was dating tried to see if she could have a happy relationship with Pablo. She had been without a partner for a long time, but Pablo continued with his lies. At one point the girl wanted to move out of where she was living. Her situation was very uncomfortable. She wanted to move into a house. Pablo offered to help her, and she believed him. He offered to withdraw money from the millions he had in the bank so he could pay the down payment on the house. The girl was so happy that she jumped for joy and spread the news to her whole family. Anyway, the process of buying the house began, knowing that these processes are long and take a while, in the course of time, one, two, six months of waiting passed, but everything seemed very doubtful.

Every day Pablo came with a different story. According to him, he had already found the house and was just waiting for the keys to be delivered. It all went around and around; the girl had already seen the house where she was supposed to be moving into and there was no reason not to believe that it wouldn't be possible. When the moment of reality arrived, they were going to move on the next day, and went to choose the furniture together and everything they needed for the moving. According to Pablo, it was going to be in two more weeks, the serious thing was when those two weeks passed.

Many questions without answers followed; unfortunately, it was another lie, the girl could not stand the situation any longer. She decided to stop by the house where she was supposed to be moving to and see what was going on, as everything had been packed. Then she got the surprise of her life, when she rang the doorbell twice, the person who opened the door was the lady who had already bought the house. Then she asked her: "Who are you? I am supposed to move into this house". The lady who opened the door answered: "I am the landlady and the owner of this house". Paul's girlfriend replied: "No way! I am supposed to move into this house in 2 weeks". And there, she fainted in front of the door, then she woke up and the lady who had already bought the house told her: "Maybe you are wrong, because I just bought this house two weeks ago".

Pablo's girlfriend was still crying, it was a very difficult situation because she could not believe it could go that far. Luckily, she was a very strong person, she got in her car and left the place, and so she arrived home with a depression that was difficult to overcome. For her it was like dying and at the same time not wanting to start again. But she still got up to keep fighting.

After two hours, Pablo showed up, but he had the suspicion that Dulce already knew everything. So, he realized what he would have to face and the embarrassment he would have to endure for such a big lie. Nevertheless, he had the nerve to continue telling lies, saying that the lady who had bought the house was lying and not to worry that he had the key, that they were different keys. However, she wasn't going to believe him anymore. She was so furious that she wanted to kill him, she grabbed the first thing she could find to smash Pablo's head. He rushed out, begging for forgiveness. Then she closed the door and started crying, trying to analyze how she was going to start over with a broken heart and no energy, with two small children who also bought the story about moving in the house. In other words, it was a complete disaster.

At the end everything was discovered, and it turned out that Pablo was completely broke. He had no money, no car, he didn't even have a place to live, he would sleep just about anywhere as nighttime arrived. He lived in his so-called reality and in his lies that no one would believe, only he himself would believe them. That's his fantasy world and unfortunately there are many others like that. Remember that it is better to tell the truth even if it hurts, than telling a lie that could end up killing you and everyone around you.

The reality and sad story of Mercedes

Since Mercedes was born, she was a little different, her hormones were more masculine, but despite that she had 4 girls. They meant everything to her, but that did not change her way of being, tastes and sexual preferences. Her life went from pause to pause, there was always something going on. She was arrested for trying to enter the United States illegally. From then on, the girls' grandparents took care of them. Mercedes was in jail for three years, that did not do her any good, because when she got out, she still had a lot of bad habits.

Mercedes disguised herself as an educated person and went to the store choosing expensive things to resell them at half price. That was her way of living and making money. She also dedicated herself to drug use, and trafficking, and through gangs she would steal money from the Narcos. Sometimes the gang members would turn into the opposite, repeatedly raping Mercedes. On many occasions there were up to three men together, until they left her for dead. She was only 4 feet 3 inches tall, but all those tragedies made Mercedes stronger. When she recovered, she sought revenge against the gang members.

Everyone knew her because she had a lot of courage, she was not afraid, she was capable of anything, and even men sought her out to feel accompanied by her. All of Mercedes' friends had criminal records, they were drug addicts, ascensions (people who climb in some way), and robbers. For several years she was using different dangerous drugs. That was not the worst of it, they made her participate in the murders that on many occasions, it was not one but several people who were victims of these murders. Mercedes had to accompany them to dig mass graves where they could bury two, three or even five dead bodies. When she had to help or witness such atrocities, in her mind she felt that she no longer wanted to do it. It was impossible because her friends made her do it anyway. If she refused, she could be the next victim. Over time, her friends began to disappear. Little by little they were murdered and found in the graves. Bodies covered with bullet holes and stab wounds.

According to her, those were the kind of deaths that they deserved. This woman's heart was untouched by the killing of all these people or anyone who crossed her path. At one point she couldn't take it anymore. Her survival experience had been so negative, it seemed like she had changed overnight. She only had two friends left; they were addicted to cocaine and heroin. She would help them find the veins, so that they could do the injections, because their body was already infected, and it would be difficult to find them. She sometimes had to do injections in their private parts, because the veins were visible in those areas. With all these experiences, Mercedes moved to another state where she supposedly started a different life. Unfortunately, she was arrested again. So far, she is serving a sentence of many years.

That's where Mercedes opened her mind and her heart. Now, she says she is at least "paying for everything she has done" and she wants to cleanse her soul. Mercedes says that on the outside, she was dead and that she feels the life that she now has, is very beautiful. She started to visit church with a desire to become a better person, so that when she comes out, she can be accepted by society. With the opportunity to not be viewed for who she was, but for who she now is.

Opportunities

When we talk about opportunities, we imagine that it is something that arrives at our door. But no, it is not like that, opportunities are something mysterious, sometimes we have them in front of us and we don't want to see them. This does not mean that it is a gift in the mail; unfortunately, we all wish it were so, rather we all believe that they are opportunities that we have earned, or that we deserve, and sometimes they are so good that we do not think they are for us, and we let them slip through our hands. (Little tips)

The opportunities that we can take in life like going to college, in this case, you can win a scholarship, but you must study hard. You can find a rich man, but you have to have personality, buy a house, for that you have to have a job, have many children but you have to be a good mother, you could find a trip opportunity, but you must have your documentation up to date, if you get a project, you have to be a good engineer, and to understand certain things, it takes a lot of effort and discipline.

There are opportunities where we should just listen and see and have a desire to become and to obtain what any human being would like to achieve in life, to feel fulfilled and not have that emptiness that does not allow us to act and achieve important things, as well as the opportunity to receive productive messages and advice.

We must know how to listen to people who have already gone through difficult situations, who try to make sure that we do not go through or suffer because of decisions like theirs. We do not listen to those things that God sends us, which are more than opportunities. If we manage to capture those gifts, they will do more than opportunities, they can avoid us many problems, and we can have a healthy and happy life, sometimes you feel that you have so much, that you can give many opportunities to others.

In your life would you like or prefer to have something that lasts? Things that you have for a short time that you have not been able to enjoy.

I exhort you, from my experience, I had everything in life and right now I cannot enjoy it, the only things I am enjoying is the material and what I was able to collect in my mind, all the positive and happy, as humans, being able to share what we will always be carrying in us, wherever we go. It's about the changes in people when they recover their lost lives. In which they were living with no life, but in a short time they see the changes. For me it was a gift that I was going to always keep with me, I call all of this "opportunity", because as a human being and with a bit of effort, it was possible to save lives, that despite of having it all, they had nothing.

Craziness

When we talk about crazy, it does not mean that we are crazy, on the contrary, there are many people who have their five senses, and do crazier things than a normal person, but there is nothing wrong with being or acting crazy. First because when you are crazy there are treatments that can help you, but when you act crazy there is no treatment, because your madness is natural and as we all know that if it is natural there is no medical treatment.

Many people act crazy, for them it's fun and they like it when someone else laughs at them, or they might do things within the natural that might not seem right to someone else, and many can avoid being judged. Anyway, madness can be mixed feelings, and they feel that somehow, they can hide their madness or show it, to hide those things that torment them, and that they themselves don't even know where they are standing.

We are talking about those who pretend to be crazy, they of course tend to be liked by some stereotypes, it means that there are many who identify with them, and somehow they get free things; for example if you find yourself in a bar you may get free drinks, gifts as material things, you can say that they have some kind of benefits, but sometimes they think that life is easier for them because of their personality, but beware! it can be double-edged sword, some people get used to some pampering, but, everything is always up to a time.

People get tired, they may help you once or twice, it could be that the third time, they do not have enough to help, then since you are already used to that kind of help, you will think that this person does not want to help you anymore but remember that you are not crazy for real.

Because just as others get the things they have, you can get them too. Do not confuse sugar with poison and be thankful for the things they did for you once; it is important to keep in mind that there are many types of craziness, for example crazy risks.

Sometimes it may take you to do something, or to talk a lot, and sometimes it is not at all serious, and if we only knew that from a madness many beautiful things could emerge, for example if your madness is about dancing and acting, or any hobby that we sometimes do not give it much importance and that actually turns into something that you always dreamed of, and that leads you to fill the emptiness which makes you act like a crazy person.

Other types of madness also include addiction, such as drinking without stopping, or being in inappropriate places which we do not immediately perceive. We must remember that any wrong movement can lead us to madness, and not being able to return to our common sense.

Confirmed story

Example of something similar and real cases that happened in 1990, Michelle Santana, was a girl with a lot of potential and charisma, everything she did seemed crazy, but her natural joy seemed to be a game. Everyone thought she was crazy, but this person had something special, she liked to get her things by her own effort, but no matter how much she did, it was unremarkable.

Because of the poverty in which she lived, and despite being cheerful and spontaneous, she knew and was very clear that it was not going to be easy. One of the things that struck her was that one day she was walking down the street in her village and a car came slowly by, and the young man was talking to her in a flattering way, trying to convince her to ride with him. Part of the things the young man was saying was that he had just arrived from New York, and he had a lot of money.

_ "Sweetheart come with me and let's have a good time." _ She looked at him and said: _ "No, just because you came from New York you think I must go with you. What is happening to you?" _ And he answered: _ "Nothing sweetheart, you are very pretty, and I want to get to know you."
She replied: "I don't think that's the right way to get to know a person, keep walking to find the one that matches up with you." _ The young man had no choice but to leave.

What a shame, only because a poor woman is seen out walking, some men think that they have the right to make all sorts of propositions, so pathetic. That gave Michelle strength and she started to think, that not because she was poor, she would be giving herself away to anyone, she chose to continue studying so that nobody would make advances to her, and she knew that the things that she wanted to accomplish would not come easy.

She was a normal and pretty girl, but she had a strange way of being, she was very spontaneous, sometimes she said things that were hard to believe. She would say things, and no one would believe her. Not because she was telling lies, but because they were things that, to a simple person, were disturbing. She gradually unraveled each one of those crazy things.

Her documents had been processed, and everything was in order. Her visa to the United States was issued. It was a challenge for her, because one cannot study only with a visa as a non-resident, and eventually she met someone. They got married, had children, she became a legalized resident and was able to go to college.

She took some courses in which she would be able work and earn a better income. In the course of time the girl that people considered crazy, and that everything that she said was a joke, was able to achieve what other regular family members could not, little by little she became a successful businesswoman.

We must not judge based on the external but rather on the capacity that each one of us may have, and even if they may seem like madness, you will always see something impressive. We should not judge but visualize the potential of each human being.

Nearby days

Berta's story and life:

After spending 10 years in prison, I was seeing my days close to my release, it was an incredible feeling just to think that I was going to see my family. At that moment it was very meaningful for me. So many things went through my head, for example, you get to think that when you have freedom you don't take advantage of it, or value what you have around you, when you lose everything, you value even the smallest thing around you; especially the fresh air, my mother's food, my father's advice and my brothers' criticism, but above all the love of my children, and all the years I wasn't with them. I lost all that when they locked me up, when the time came for me to leave, I felt as if I was almost born again, finding the most beautiful thing that God could give me as a human being, the family.

But, above all, the plans I was going to make when I was free. To be able to continue with my studies, and the things that fill my life that I always wanted to have before I went to prison. But you don't think about those things until after you make the mistakes, that's how I spent the 80 days I had left, I went out and my whole family was waiting for me outside, it was an unexplainable experience, I felt so much happiness at that instant. A moment that I cannot change for anything or anyone; and even if you have nothing, you are and feel super lucky to see your own people supporting you and wanting to see you happy. I have seen many cases that even though they know the consequences they don't care. And even if you commit many atrocities that can lead you to serve many years in prison; we must create awareness, that not only we suffer but also the people who love us, and keep in mind that everything you worked for can be lost in seconds, that means that all your efforts were in vain. When you get out it is more difficult to recover and start again. As a proverb says: It is better to have a little and make it appear as a lot; and not to have a lot and make it appear as a little in seconds. But it's not about how much or how little, it's about feeling that physical and spiritual peacefulness; and there is no money that can buy that. I agree that ambition will always exist, and we only awake when we are in trouble; and even then, we do not stop or change, causing our current and future destruction, if only we would take a moment and analyze that what comes easy, goes easy. With the difference that when we work, we value our money more by having good management.

The title of the intensity of human feelings has a lot to do with this topic, since, if we consider all that we must go through, and the time you waste in jail and compare it to a before and an after, I will never trade the before for the after. That after is the one you never want to remember, but it is always good to remember it, because it will help us not to make the same mistakes of the past. This topic was also inspired, for all those people who can read this book, know that I was involved in heavy fights, I was hungry, I was cold, I could not communicate with any of my relatives, and visits were restricted, and my friends forgot about me.

So, the days, months, and years became longer, but fortunately the one who was always with me was my Lord Jesus Christ who gave me the strength and energy to survive so much anguish and anxiety, which caused me nausea, diarrhea, and tremors in my body, as well as eating my nails until I pulled them out and drew blood. All these anxieties and nightmares that I lived through at night, there was no pill or medicine that could help me. Only my father Jesus Christ gave me the strength to survive until my time of departure, and to be able to carry in my heart, the hope and love to all those who never forgot me.

The lie and the shield

The lie and the shield have something in common; with the shield you cover during the fights with knives and the lion's bites. And with the lies you cover yourself and save yourself from any situation you are going through. We compare it with the shield because it covers you for a long or short time.

When the time is short, there are more possibilities of being able to fix the problem with less consequences. But when the lies are being used for a long time, the consequences can be fatal.

Observation:

When one of us is lying for whatever reason, we should keep in mind what the result was, or how much it helped us at the time. And observe how many consequences it can bring us in the future. If we need the present more than the future, this will help us to make practical decisions; and if we are people who only think about the present, it means that we have no plans.

Scene:

There was a group of people who worked in a very prestigious company, this group was formed by employees with different functions within the company, each one put ideas to fulfill the purpose. Which was to work for 23 years, and make believe that everything was fine in accounting, to carry out the theft of 10 million dollars. And of course, with that they had their future assured, at that moment they did not think about the consequences, and when it was discovered, everything that had been planned for so long was going to end It turns out that the ambition to believe that everything was going to work out well, and to feel that the certainty gained boldness at that moment, and what was intended, perhaps was never going to be obtained, but it fills you with courage and the only thing your instinct dictates, is to get it done, especially if you have the support of your peers.

Judging:

At the moment when everything is finished, and it is your turn to distribute the money, there is always something that is not going to go well, whether it is nerves or feelings of guilt, envy, happiness. So, there are many uncertainties, and when they look at each other's faces, at that moment, they ignore each other's intentions. Then each one takes his money and leaves the place, but each one is thinking if this happiness that he has at that moment is going to last forever, since each one is going to live a different life, and it turns out that each one of them has a different family, and some of them are going to be questioned. Others have friends who in one way or another are going to be envious; and that's when they will judge you for your drastic change of lifestyle.

Interpretation:

To all these people we can comment that lies only give us more problems. They may satisfy you for a while, but in the course of time they will bring you a lot of pain and problems. Although at that moment the shield protects you, remember that not all the time you will be fighting, and when you neglect the enemies will come, and all the negative things that surround you from the moment you started your own audacity, of wanting to have something, that the only thing you can do is to be happy for a moment, but if you think about it and analyze it, you have to remember that when you are discovered the shield is taken away from you. Your life would change from 100% to 5% of happiness, when you have to spend years and years in jail, for wanting to have something that does not belong to you, and wanting to have the lifestyle of a millionaire; knowing that in a few minutes you will live worse than one of those who sometimes have nothing and it is difficult for them to eat or have what is necessary as a human being to survive.

My favorite hobby, club night

Since I was 10 years old, I discovered my passion for music, not because I know how to sing but because I like to dance, and I felt that as I grew older, I liked it more and more, until little by little I was creating my own choreography, my own movements, which made me feel super good. It was like getting out of my body, an incredible adrenaline rush. At first, I thought I was going to get over it, but it wasn't like that, I got better and better, and despite having my children I never stopped, I always did it like the first time.

I always had problems with my partner, he didn't want me to dance, not because he didn't like it but because he was jealous, I told him that he was something stronger than me. So, I decided, I had to have a disco style room made in my house; that way I could please my husband and make both of us happy. But of course, it was not the same as doing it by myself. I needed all the energy of other people, or with friends that one meets in the nightclub. Even if it meant getting in trouble with my husband.

Sometimes when I met girls younger than me, they would come up to me and tell me that they wanted to dance like me, of course, I felt special, considering that I wasn't doing it to impress but because I felt great, my style was different. My motivation was Cher and Madonna, two beautiful women who despite the years look like 20-year-old girls. I got motivated and followed through with a firm goal, because I felt it was what made me happy.

Interpretation:
We all have a favorite hobby. We must consider that it

can be a point of motivation for our lives, and even if we can't do it at a professional level we should not give up and always remember how difficult it is to be happy. And if we discover that we can achieve it, even with a lot of effort and sacrifice, it is important because in that way we can project happiness to others, and to the people who are around us, no matter what kind of hobby it is.

If you like to sing around the house, do it. If you like to work after work, do it. Maybe it's something our partner likes. And if you like to race cars, buy a cart, prepare it little by little and go for a run. Anyway, these are examples for you to follow the instincts that make you happy; and not wait for someone to bring you your happiness. Remember that everyone is looking for the same thing.

Ñoñi La distinguida

Champions

Thanks to my son Jamaine Ortiz, he was the one who wrote the first pages when he was only 14 years old, he was, and is a model child, he wanted to give an example to all the children of his age, and to us as adults, he was my inspiration. He says his dream is to have his own gym and train kids like him. And so, they can feel motivated to keep going and be children with projections to the future, who have confidence in themselves, just like him, because he was 6 years old when he started. His motivation is to continue until the end.

JAMAINE ORTIZ

JAMAINE ORTIZ

Credit to Bill Doyle, Telegram Copyright ©

In the main event, Ortiz (10-0, 5 KOs) will defend his WBC junior world title against Brazil's Vitor Jones (15-4, 9 KOs) in an eight-round bout.

Ortiz, 22, won his title on February 23 in Twin River by an eight-round unanimous decision over Ricardo Quiros of Oxnard, California. Quiros was 10-0.

The Doherty High graduate joined Chad Dawson and Matt Remillard as the third CES boxer to capture a WBC youth title, open to boxers 23 and under.

Ortiz also became the first Worcester boxer to capture a junior world title. Jones has 15 wins and 4 defeats, with nine knockouts, but all four of his losses have been by KO.

Jones, 25, had lost four of his last six fights. His first two losses came by first round knockout.

And he lost his last two fights by third-round technical knockout, to 17-1 Sebastien Bouchard on Dec. 1 and 9-0 Enriko Gogokhia on Feb. 2.

Contact Bill Doyle at william.

doyle@telegram.com.

Follow him on Twitter.

@BillDoyless.

Miracles and testimonies

Our lives are full of miracles, things that are hard to believe, always happen to us, and we think that these happen by coincidence, they are things that perhaps we do not deserve, and if we were to meditate, this world is a miracle, and even more so to live in it. Other miracles we have are cured of terminal illnesses people, and many people are saved from fatal accidents, many survive beatings and on the other hand many when they are drowning, first aid is applied, and they manage to survive. We also go through all these traumas, and we have triumphs in life, such as jobs, fame, university degrees, and we can call them miracles, because we were able to get out of the trauma in which we lived.

For example, to be a thief and stop being a thief is a miracle, to be in prison and get out of prison is a miracle, to use drugs and get out of addiction is a miracle, to be a murderer and stop being a murderer is a miracle. So, we create awareness of all the risks that every human being is exposed to, getting up every day is the most beautiful miracle. If we see it as a miracle of God, things can be easier, because if miracles did not exist, all those temptations could be determinant, and we would not believe that life would not give us another chance to complete the purpose with which we were born.

God gave us the right to make our own decisions and we do it in our own way, but for everything there are consequences and sometimes we do not have enough capacity to accept them. There is a miracle that I want to share, since for anyone who hears the story, it may be unbelievable, they could see it as something positive or negative. It was a girl named Nadia, she was pregnant, but she had an addiction to a drug called crystal meth. This drug was so strong that it took away her hunger, to the point of not wanting to eat at any time. Crystal was her breakfast, lunch, and dinner, and she stayed that way until she was seven months pregnant. Just imagine a seven-month pregnancy that has only received smoke.

What can you expect when the baby is born? At In the midst of the anguish and anxiety of using such an addictive drug, one night she went to her room crying, saying, "My God, if it is true that you exist, take away this addiction that is going to kill me and my baby, and who knows, maybe he is already dead.

And she says that the next day, she woke up drinking milk and eating food. She felt a breeze blowing across her face, and the rest of her body, a week after she felt a little relieved from the drugs, her pregnancy continued to develop, because during her seventh month, she still had not noticed her pregnancy. She managed to have the baby at eight and a half months, a girl was born. They did the medical exams, and she was very healthy. Something completely unbelievable, anyone who knew her story would not believe it.

There was also another pregnant woman who was planning to have an abortion, and at that time she fell into a coma, but then she had her baby. Giving her mother the happiness that for many years she thought did not exist. These are the incredible and important miracles that God shows us through our lives, and to understand that happiness is not given to us by destiny, it is created by our own actions when something unforeseen happens to us. There is the miracle of hope that makes us be born again.

Dying and being born

We human beings, rather believers, know that we all must die, but it doesn't even cross our minds. And to be born again, in the reality of the world we are in, we have not seen it. Because to tell the truth, to die and to be born, for many of us, is to die with time. To be born again is what we would really like, because we know that in the eyes of all religions we die, so we can reach the kingdom of heaven, that is, if you are saved, in the eyes of God; you will be saved, that is eternal life; the theme of dying and being born originated during the course of the years of life of a lady named Bela.

She was able to define the subject (to die and to be born) by the things that happened to her and that it is possible that it happens to many, but they cannot assimilate it with some sense. Bela was a 40-year-old lady, but since she was 10 years old, she had real visions, and when she let the public know it, anyone could think that she was crazy. The vision consisted of her being dead for hours and waking up in another place with many people who had never met with her before in the world she lived in. And in her heart, she felt that seeing all those faces was as if they were real people. People she had seen before.

When she saw them and talked to them, she even looked for resemblances in some of her family members. She felt something very unusual. But it had happened to her several times, she didn't pay attention to it and sometimes she thought she was going crazy. When she woke up from her visions and tried to forget them and realize that she never had those predictions, it was that she was not going to be with her real family, but when she had the opportunity to see the birth of her son, the prize was a new birth of a child that she did not expect. That kept her alive for the surprise that she was going to bring to her family. And when she came back from death, the birth allowed her to stay alive, almost for a full year. Because everything was to die and at the same time to be born double. She was able to discover the reason for her visions, the dreams came true in the real world. No one was content and they all seemed dead and wandering around the house. Bela was able to understand the work that God had done in her and what she had to go through; she could finally believe and live; everyone in the house was happy, and everyone was living a very different life.

After living through all these processes and being able to clear her mind, she understood that things happen for a reason in life. Bela went on with her normal life raising her children fighting for them, and in the course of time what had to happen happened. Destiny had something in store for her that neither she nor her family expected. She was not going to be around for a year, she was not going to be present for her children or her family. It was like being dead at that moment, and as if she was being transferred to another small world where the human population was approximately 1,500 people.

It was like dying and being born. In a place she did not know, but the strange thing was that each of the people around her, for her were family, neighbors, and friends that she had seen before, and instead of feeling strange with all that situation it was like being in family again, even though her real family was not present. Now I can understand the beginning and the end of our life; she on her part can say that the end of the story is that she is living a life in peace, with her new family on earth because with her experience it is better to die and be born than to die spiritually and mentally.

Motivation

Motivation is what pushes us to move forward, and to understand that we need to be motivated from an early age and during growth. So much so that there are children who cry a lot when they are little, and their mother sings a song or plays music and the child calms down. We as human beings have ups and downs, it has nothing to do with age or because we have a disease, many times we let ourselves be carried away by the little desire to do something, even if it is productive sometimes, we do not care.

Example:

I was working where there were 1,500 women in discipline rehab, and they all had a story to tell, and each story was to either raise or lower their self-esteem completely. But it all depends on what your motivations are and analyze how you can fulfill your moral and spiritual feelings. Example: if you are a 20-year-old it is logical that you have more energy than a 30- or 40-year-old, right? but when I was in that place, I could see that the ladies who were 30 and 40 had more energy than the 20-year-old girls; we all wondered why?

Interpretation:

The 20-year-olds believe that because of their age they can achieve everything, and that life is not going to end for them. And the 30- and 40-year-olds want to look like 20-year-olds. There is nothing wrong with that, but the motivation of the 30- and 40-year-olds was to fulfill their desire to live and do what they never did when they had all the possibilities, they realized how restricted they were, doing the impossible to achieve their goals and finish school. For me it was the most beautiful thing among women, because in my 20s I was able to live all these experiences and could talk to all of them, and they were motivated by the following answers, some said: "I want to be a better person", "I want my family to be proud of me". Others said: "when I got here, I weighed 200 pounds and now being motivated I lost 50 pounds, because I always wanted to have my beautiful body and I thought I was never going to achieve it, sometimes I looked at myself and I could not believe it, and that motivated me to continue".

It is a pity that many do not believe in anything, they only think in negative things that only destroy them, nevertheless, time goes by and they will realize that when they want to achieve something it will cost them more because time goes by, that is why it is good to pamper yourself and always motivate yourself, no matter if you are fat, skinny or petite and remember that if you have a good personality, good presence and good conversation and you are a compatible human being, it will not matter your color or your size; What will matter is the value that you have acquired in times that God gave you the opportunity to achieve part of your purpose, that will get you where you want to be and be able to feel very confident and do things that you feel proud of, around you.

Do not get carried away because we are young, we must take advantage of time, that is why we live different stages in life, to learn from them, not them from us. And even though all the things we achieve in our lives are memories and presents that will only bring us happiness and love to give away. But if you don't do your discipline correctly you will only live frustrated and you will not feel alive, since you will not have love or affection for anything.

Nationalities

Nationality is belonging to a certain country. Each nationality is a different world. They have different rules, different ways of living and sharing. But everyone walks in their own world, virtual and spiritual. They pass you by and you see them every day. At airports, when you travel from one country to another. It's nice, as human beings we like to know different cultures, and learn from them. But when you must live with so many people close to you. sometimes you must share a house or a room with many of them. For example, black, white, Latino, and from all countries.

Some get along well, but others can be disruptive, poisonous, inconsiderate, and complicated. Sometimes we feel like we are in an anthill, because in many of the cases we have no other option to survive constantly and silently, hoping for a miracle to be able to have a normal life, in the human sense because of the situation you live in. If we see it in a different way... it is so nice to want to share with different nationalities, learn from them, and see in many of them that they are educational and constructive, because we are all human, and we should not live killing each other like cats and dogs.

Example: a country like the Dominican Republic with so many natural beauties, that has many touristic places, wherever you go, and you meet people from different countries, enjoying together in harmony.

Dominicans like to share and learn from them, we treat foreigners as if they were family, our communication, food, and hospitality, is one of the most visited islands and considered by tourists, they like to go on vacation and enjoy the beauty and wonders it has, because of the reception that we Dominicans offer them. We do not notice or devalue if you are black, white, or Latino. We treat you as if you belong to our country. These are the things that make us recognize that we cannot live without each other, We all need each other, and even if at first one does not agree, we can all live in peace and help each other.

Ñoni La Distinguida

Childhood

This was a boy named Pedro, and a girl named Lucia. All children are curious, but these two kids liked to experiment a lot; Pedro and Lucia got to playing, daddy and mommy, and ended up having sex. These kids were only 14 years old, the girl got pregnant. She decided to have her child, it was a boy, but before the child was born, they wanted to make Pedro's father responsible for the child, but the mother of the father of the child that was going to be born decided to take charge, for that they had to go to court, and all those complications to be able to adopt the child.

First, they took the child in front of the judge, who saw and could not believe it, it was just a girl. The judge was thinking that it had been an adult who had raped her, he asked them to look for the person to make him responsible for his crime, and that was when they took the child's father, and it was discovered that he was a 14-year-old teenager.

Childhood can be very complicated, no matter where you live or what nationality you are, if you come from a rich or poor family, or if you are from the countryside. But if you are from the city I imagine you are curious to know the difference of these already mentioned; the truth is that when you are a child, you don't know what future awaits you, for example, if you are rich or the son of rich parents, as a child you have that in your mind and you think that is the life you deserve or that all people are born rich, but when you realize that there are differences, then that's when the complications begin. If you need to force yourself to study and have a career. Also, when you are a child, you start to compete at school, if you arrive by car or if you arrive walking. And that's when unnecessary imaginations are created in your mind. But not all children are the same, some are kind, and even if they are rich, they like to spend time with those who are poor. That's when the child begins to remember some of the things that their parents taught them. For example, not to be racist, that not all people are equal, and that not all of us are lucky enough to be rich or financially comfortable. A poor child suffers a lot, but sometimes they don't understand why they are poor.

They also don't understand when other children make fun of them. Many go back to their parents and tell them what happened, then the parents say don't worry my child, there is nothing wrong with being poor, God wanted us to be that way, but if you study, you can be like them someday; the truth is that some children listen to the advice, but others don't, and say "I don't want to be poor". They start doing inappropriate things that in the end will not benefit them in the future. They may get money fast, and pretend with other children, but many of them end up in the juvenile courts, where the real problem of youth begins, it haunts them until they are adults.

Also, when they are country kids, they have a humility and are more sensitive, compared to city kids. But, even if they are from the city or the village, it doesn't matter, if you have the will to fight, to study, you can achieve things and it doesn't matter if you are poor or rich, or where you come from. When you are an adult, you understand the importance of life. As a child you have the opportunity and the ability to decide what you want to do in life, you can become a doctor, a priest, an engineer, the truth is that the decisions and the ability with which you do each of the things, will determine in time or before time. Define your feelings, what you really want, be happy and make other human beings happy.

I don't want to lose you

There are many ways to not want to lose a person, but "I don't want to lose you", includes making many sacrifices. It is "not wanting to lose", if it is not being able to use the necessary weapons to "not lose" that loved one. And if you do lose him or her, it is because he or she was never yours. Holding someone by force is not healthy at all, it creates false illusions that sooner or later fade away, leaving a profound emptiness in the depths of the soul. It happens to many of us, that we wait and wait, and for a long time we get nothing, as there are also many, who get things without having to wait or asking for them.

Sounds like a very nice reality! I am talking about those people with diabolical instincts, that take advantage of the ingenuousness, no matter the age, nor the sex of their innocence. These were cases of real-life events of a little girl named Francheska. Although she is now an adult, when she was 5 years old, she was being abused by a family member, and he kept threatening her all the time. She could not speak, and her mother had died when she was 3 years old, so she had to stay with an aunt, the aunt's husband abused the girl every day, offering her slimming pills, since he only called her fat and ugly, damaging her mind, and he would seduce her constantly.

When she turned 16 years old it was difficult to comprehend or assimilate so many atrocities for such an innocent being, and although the aunt knew it, she kept quiet, since she did not want to lose her husband. She preferred to sacrifice the child rather than lose the person she considered she loved and keep him by her side, without caring about the suffering of an innocent being, and like this case, there are many people who know about the problem and do nothing out of fear of being left. The sad thing is that in this person's life there is only evil. We ask ourselves, what do you prefer, to remain silent for so many years or to speak, even if you must escape, or do you prefer to remain silent and continue to suffer for the rest of your life due to the fear of being attacked. We must know that there are always ways out of the problem, we just must be a little strong, not let another person destroy us.

There are many ways to be destroyed. In the case of this little girl, from childhood to adulthood she was always using drugs, regardless of all the good things around her, and on certain occasions she had the opportunity to escape and did not. These are the necessary tools to get to know more deeply, the people you don't want to lose. Example, if you have a friend treat them as just your friend. If you have a boyfriend, love him, and treat him as your husband.

If you have a brother, make him feel like he is your only one. If you have a father and mother, make them feel that you are the best child. These are the examples that could avoid conflicts to not end up losing a loved one. Let us pray day and night, but, above all, let us have our feelings clear and defined.

Boyfriends

The word boyfriends can have many meanings. You could be dating a classmate, a co-worker, and you get along well with that person, and little by little you start to fall in love and miss them when they are not by your side. The most beautiful love you can experience is when you are 14 or 15 years old. I remember that I had a boyfriend when I was 14 years old, for me, he was my prince charming. He was a super handsome boy, slim, white, very elegant.

His clothes fit him as if he were a magazine model, in other words, a real prince. Sometimes my eyesight would get puzzled, and I didn't want to stop looking at him. When he would disappear around the street corners, I couldn't wait to see him again. At that time, we were just spending time together and getting to know each other, and he would treat me like a queen.

I liked it when he would leave work, we would play in the park, and my mind would always tell me that he was my love, that I never wanted him to leave my side. But as they say, not everything lasts forever. Eventually the relationship ended, but I was still in love with him.

I was studying high school and he was going to college. I remember that I would stay for hours waiting for him to get out of class just to see him from afar. But I didn't want him to see me, I didn't want him to think I was spying on him.

When I got to see him from afar it was like seeing God in front of me. I was happy for the rest of the day. I also cried a lot because he was my first love. I didn't understand why we couldn't be together, but later I understood and discovered that his parents didn't want him to be with me. They influenced him a lot, they always questioned what kind of family and level I had. In other words, practically in many cases, it doesn't matter how much love you feel for someone, because many people only care about material things.

For me it was a very nice experience, but the most beautiful thing was to know that choosing was not a matter of losing or winning; life goes on and if someone is not by your side or does not love you as you love them, retaliating against that person, is not a choice.

On the contrary when you love someone, let them fly away, that's my theory, because if you try to keep them by your side it's not true love. If that love comes back to you, it's because it was always there, and it never left from your heart. After that cute love story, my heart was hardening, but what I could never change was my way of thinking.

I mean that when it is about a pure and true love, the opposite of when it is about romantic love for a woman or any other person, is to give help without expecting anything in return, and if you expect something in return it is not a true feeling. If you ever feel that way about someone, it means that you are confused and at that moment you don't know what you want.

You must try to overcome the damage you do to yourself by the time you waste on each other. Nor should we be thinking so much about materialism, that is not what makes us happy; of course, it is true that it helps a lot. You must consider how sweet a person is, and how they treat you. Also, the time he/she dedicates to you and your family.

We know that sometimes we get tired, and we think we are going to be happy, and it is not so, the person wants to live as if he/she was still single. Then one wonders if it is worth rushing into any kind of relationship, just because it suits us, without thinking about the consequences because we are illusioned, and that illusion ends in disillusionment....

Message:
When you have a love relationship that makes you happy in that moment, or you are living what you have never lived before, try to make the most of it.
There are many love relationships that are like the wind, that run away leaving fragrance of pain, and a bitterness difficult to erase, and you must start again, so, HELLOOOO!

Losing and winning

When we talk about losing or winning, we always think of things. When we talk about losing something, what we think of first, is about losing money or something material, it is the same thing. That does not mean that if we gain something material, we should know that we would rather prefer to lose material things, than the things that hurt us so much.

We don't even remember that we could have had it once in our life. Sometimes we lose something deeper, such as a loved one or our life or waste time on something that is not worth it. As well as investing time in things that can destroy you. That destruction can last for a long period and that is when you think about the loss you really had.

Losing one of your family members, children, love relationship, or immigration documents. those are very difficult to recover. We say: God, how am I going to recover the time? It is said that the time that has already passed, does not come back, and to make up for it is very complicated. Sometimes we think, I would have to die and be born again to take advantage and do things better than before, trying to do what I could not do in the time when I had the opportunity to do it.

It is important to act very cautiously, when we can recover what we've lost, not trying to do everything at the same time. We must let everything happen step by step; we know that desperation is part of failure. If we do not do it that way, it is possible that we will end up making other mistakes even though we know the consequences. As we have seen in many cases, we lose everything. When we make a mistake and end up in prison it is obvious that we are not doing things right. Sometimes we need a space where we can think and be ready to live in the community and serve our own. Sometimes being close to a family member does not mean we are doing good; on the contrary, our mind is empty and with nothing to offer. That's why when we are in a recovery facility, we realize how much we gain. You get ready to learn to miss your loved ones and value what you didn't care about before.

If you don't value yourself, you can't love others, those feelings of guilt begin to heal little by little. That's when you say, my God, thank you for all that you have given me and all that I have learned. Now I feel ready to have and appreciate all the things I didn't care about before.

I feel that the time lost was more like time gained, because if gaining is believing that you lost what you had, when you didn't even know that you had it, instead of a lost, look at it in a way of many gains.

Interpretation:
We must always see that to win, we will go through certain processes. If you analyze or self-analyze, you may never have to lose everything. On the contrary, when you lose something, you will have gains, because you will take advantage of every minute and every hour. Minutes and hours will become eternal gains.

Who you really are

All the time you think you know yourself, but a lot of unexplainable things happen around you. Everything goes wrong and you think you have bad luck, but it is not bad luck that drives your destiny. It is important to know who we are, the memories that we lived when we were children, those memories that cover your mind and you could not overcome, unfortunately it is something that you are going to carry with you to the point that it is already part of your life. And if you did not overcome it then your personality is going to be covered by that past.

Of course, we are talking about how you lived your life as a child, your life as a teenager, and your life as an adult. And if there is something from childhood that left you frustrated that you have not been able to forget, your adolescent life could not be the same.

If you had lived a healthy childhood surrounded by lots of love, and if we fail to overcome the difficult and transform the negative into something positive, when we reach adulthood, it becomes very difficult to overcome. It also happens when you create bad habits, that will always be part of your life. So that's when those questions come, who you really are, where we create different personality types, one day you're happy and another day you're unhappy.

These are stages where you want to explore all kinds of schemes that can destroy you. Like an illegal business, drug use, theft, you don't want to work, and despite all our defects we believe we deserve everything, and we don't get anything. We human beings get tired, although we want to help, we don't want to be helped. We do not understand that we are human beings against each other, and none of us is super gifted. They lived that and never got over it and now as adults they explain those attitudes, but others do not accept it and they feel rejected and bullied. There comes a time when they suffer among themselves, which many do not understand the reason why they are rejected, they feel alone, but even though they are to blame, they start blaming others.

They do not understand that they need to change all the negative things for which others do not want to spend time with them or even be around them.

Interpretation:
If you give something don't expect anything in return. If someone shows you friendship show the same, if someone listens to you, listen to them too, if someone gives you a word of encouragement don't act as if you were angry. Some of us have doctrines, skills, habits, experience, but above all patience, and what we want is to help and make people feel that life is a gift from God, which we do not know how to take advantage of. We think we live alone.

Experience
I had the opportunity to meet people of all kinds, and despite all my problems, I tried to understand their sorrows and sufferings. But the curious thing was that they did not realize the mistakes they made. They would get involved in many wrong confusions where they didn't understand why they were suffering, and strange things would happen to them with their friends, and when trying to help them survive and do different things, they would discover that the problem was more serious than they thought. When they were younger, they were envious and when they were teenagers they would get involved in fights.

Observation:

To all this, I could notice that one of those people with problems that I was helping spiritually and mentally, was able to admit their imperfections.

I noticed the difference in his change, he no longer lied, if he acted badly, he apologized, he visited the church for the first time, and then he went twice a week. It was very important when he could recognize that his behavior was not going to lead him to be a happy person, and he said he wanted to be a person like me, but I answered him, no one can be like anyone else, we must be ourselves, with the difference of wanting to be better people.

When you see someone who doesn't deserve your attention, do it anyway, so you will know who you really are.

Remembrance of a son who forgot about his mother

Hello beautiful son, it is a pleasure for me to be able to tell you what I feel and remember all the beautiful moments we shared together. I remember when we shared your moments of accomplishments, when your dad did not attend any of them. Being the father and mother is the most beautiful thing that could happen to me in life.

I hope and wish that you will be a happy person, and that you will be strong when it is your turn to live through the most difficult moments; remember what I had to live through, thank God, I was able to overcome. I know that we are not together because of destiny, but the most important thing is that you have not forgotten me. Thank you for all the letters I have received from you, with the drawings you do at school.

The hearts of love that a son makes for his mother that he loves and misses so much. May my God repay you and forgive you, whatever you are doing at this moment, I hope they are not negative things. Remember all the things we lived together and could still live.

Memories

Many times, so many beautiful things happen to us, and we don't even give importance to them. We don't think about the need for them. When remembering them, sometimes we say or think; that's why I am like that, because when I was little, I liked to do that, or my parents did it or saw it. Although in those times we didn't give it importance, but now that we remember it, we would like to live it again or be children again. But for all people there are memories and different stages, it does not have to be only when we were children, as well as the memories in which you lived and did not take pictures; or maybe with the person who we lived it with, they do not remember it.

Who knows, reading this book may bring back memories to some of them, and they may be able to visualize what they lived with you. Maybe we are going through a difficult time, and suddenly we remember things which can cause us to smile, when perhaps, we had not been able to do so in a while. Let's start to con contemplate the memories when we were children, and we were two or three years old. I remember my parents going out partying and carrying me in their arms in those days.

They didn't have a car, and they would walk to the place where they were going to go to, with their friends, they would spend the whole night dancing. I remember that when my dad would take a bath, he would always look for the towel and soap. I also remember when he came out of the bathroom, he would sit at the table to eat. He would say to me: "Come sweetheart, sit on my lap, so you can eat with me. When he saw me eating, he would get up from the table to prepare my favorite juice. I remember when I fought with my sisters because neither one of us wanted to run errands, all the time my mom sacrificed herself working to buy us new clothes, how hard my dad had to work to feed us. I also remember my older brother helping my dad so that all my little brothers and sisters could be well and that we could go to school, also when my grandma would save my favorite food for me, when my grandpa would sing to me, I would ride on his lap and he would sing to me the "Caballito solo" song, and when my grandpa would sing the "Caballito solo" song to me, and when my grandma would sing to me, just to see me laugh.

Likewise, on the weekends we all got together as neighbors to have a good time, as well as to make plans. I remember when the oldest girl wanted to have a boyfriend, and those who already had one, the younger girls in the neighborhood spied on them, all the suitors I had at school, and it was hard for me to decide on one of them. How about when I would run away from school to go eat empanadillas or ice cream; when I would walk through the streets and boys wanted to ride me in their cars, when I would lie to my mom to go to the beach with my friends, and also stay at the beach until midnight; letting the sand take me with all the waves until I got lost in the darkness of the night.

Memories of that time I stayed until the wee hours of the morning, and then went back to the hotel with the excuse that I had gotten lost. I loved to get pretty to go out with my friends to the club and leave my boyfriend standing up, once my boyfriend found me with my friends and slapped me thinking I was with someone else, my friend threatened my boyfriend for disrespecting me, and they beat each other up. One of the hardest moments, I was dancing with my boyfriend, and they started shooting with guns, we had to run and hide in the bushes in fear of dying that night. When I was 18, I got an entrepreneur boyfriend, and he took me to his beach house so he could be the first one in my intimate life.

Because I was exploring, I wanted to look for a boyfriend on the internet; at that time the boy only showed his face in pictures, he looked very good. When I met him, he didn't want to get out of the car, and I wanted to understand why. I could see he weighed about 400 pounds, and he didn't want me to see him like that.

I remember the dance competitions with the girls at the disco, where they all wanted to do the same thing, I did. I remember when my sisters and I, we would get together and share a lot of our secrets, the ones we didn't think we were capable of doing. One of my sisters and I went on vacation and on the second stopover we caught different flights; but the nice thing was that we arrived at the same time to the place. Also, when one of my sisters visited her boyfriend instead of him visiting her, as he thought he was the woman and my sister thought she was the man. It comes to my mind, when I remarried, I felt like it was the first time. I was the happiest woman in the world because of all my husband's actions.

So many memories, like when I would go to the store and buy everything I wanted with my husband's money, all the flowers he would bring me home, and at work, my boss would get jealous and end up breaking them. I remember all the opportunities I missed and the ones I never took advantage of, thinking that I could have them at any moment. As they say, opportunities come and go, and you must take advantage of them. I remember the many times I drowned in a glass of water and found out there was no need for it. Many times, everyone judged me without knowing my feelings and sufferings, when I was more dead than alive. Despite everything I was able to stand up against all odds, put my feet on the ground and walk again. I remember the moment when I was blind and only thought about luxuries and vanities. I woke up and opened my eyes, I realized that the most important thing is to give love.

All vanities can be turned in five minutes, earthquakes, tornadoes, tsunamis, and torrential lavas. All these memories lead us to think about the vanities and the inhumanity in us. We just must keep our eyes wide open because from one minute to the next you can have them closed.

Resignation

Resignation is to conform to what is happening around you without trying or being able to do anything to change it. Sometimes we don't change it because we believe too much in fate. In my case, it is difficult for me to resign myself. I have put everything on the line to have a good future, and for my children and close relatives to have a good future as well.

I mean to put it all on the line with our sweat and a lot of effort and perseverance. Not to let life play with us, but to play with it. I mean when something negative happens to us, see it as something positive. Not to die with the problem you are going through at that moment. If we let ourselves get carried away by that, we will never get up.

We are always going to have problems, adversities, and crossroads where we must make decisions, fall, or get up. It is easy to fall, but it is not easy to get up, since at that moment the depression is so deep that we do not know if we are alive or dead. To get up we need to be alive; that's the point. When we are going through these disastrous moments, we must realize that it is something normal.

To think that there is no evil that will last 100 years, nor a body that could endure it. In my case, I did not think that way. I had a marvelous experience, so much so that I felt that my life changed completely. Although I did not believe in destiny, I also understood that destiny is made by oneself; for that reason, I did not have to resign myself to any of my mistakes. On the contrary, I had to face it and destroy the problem to start a new life.

Scene of a lived experience:

This was a lady named Ulah and another lady whose name was Rafaela. In the case of Mrs. Ulah, she lived in a field, a very mysterious woman. Her way of being frightened the children when they passed in front of her house, on their way to school. She frightened them because instead of looking like a woman, Mrs. Ulah looked like a man. She picked up pieces of coal and painted a beard and mustache on her face, and the eyebrows too.

At the same time, she talked to herself, not because she was crazy, but because when she mashed her coffee with pestle she enjoyed singing and talking to herself. The mysterious thing was that, although she was a lonely woman, we all realized that she was a very positive woman, even though the children were afraid of her. Still, Mrs. Ulah was not resigned to her ways. Every day she painted her face with black charcoal.

After a while, Mrs. Ulah made herself known to all the people of the village. Indeed, they could see that she was a very lonely lady. A woman resigned to living by being the man and woman of the house. She said she had no luck with men, for that reason she decided to feel and look like a man. She was a complete woman, only that she decided to have a double life, due to her suffering for the absence of her husband; a sad story because he was found drowned in a river near her house.

In the case of Mrs. Rafaela, I could not believe the situation she was going through. She looked and resembled my grandmother in every way. Mrs. Rafaelita was about 70 years old, and she was super admirable. She told me that she spent many years in jail for something she did not do. She was charged with conspiracy because she had been married to someone who trafficked with the Mexican cartels. She no longer had anything to do with him since she was already divorced. Even so, she was sentenced to 6 years in prison. Rafaelita had no choice but to face her sentence. She said she felt as if she was living at home.

When she was locked up, she thought a lot about Jesus Christ and the sacrifice they made her go through, without thinking about the evil they were doing to her; but rather about the experience she was going to share with her family. In this case all the negativity about Mrs. Rafaela turned into something positive.

An example on how to continue without a reason for useless resignations that, after all, when you have difficult moments, you don't have any other alternatives, but to confront them in different ways.

When we see these examples in other people, facing them in a convincing way. Keeping in mind that there is something better ahead. All this is what makes us feel that we are alive with the desire to continue sharing the world of the living that we are ourselves; even though many of us feel dead.

Feelings and actions

At my early age when I felt I had the use of reason, I saw how my family tried to survive with 10 children, and how they struggled to feed us, sometimes it was impossible to put food on the table, we had to eat not very nutritious things, the important thing was that we survived, but there came a time when they could no longer cope with so many children.

Our parents decided to send us to different places, I mean to a house where we had better possibilities, for my parents it was a lot of suffering, because sometimes they had to send us to houses without knowing the fate that awaited us; they did it little by little with the older children, I remember that the first to leave was my brother Jesus, when he looked into our eyes you could see the sadness, knowing that because of the situation they were forced to go to another city to have a better future. I am talking about the 80's, at that time my brother was just a young boy, he was the second of my older siblings; in total there were 4 boys in the family and 6 girls.

The rest of us stayed with our parents, and little by little they found a place where they could send us. They found a place for my sister Maria and another of my sisters; the sad thing was that the family was separating, and it was no longer the same, my parents were sad, and my siblings too.

My brother Jesus visited us every Sunday, you could see the joy in his eyes, and with a desire to help, so that we would all be happy. But at that time, it was impossible, since he was just getting by, and was trying to survive; but despite that his desire was so great that the little he could get, he shared it with us on holidays. I would buy gifts for my grandmother and my mom, and one or another thing for all my sisters. One day, one cloudy afternoon, with light rain, someone came from the city with the bad news that my brother had been in a tragic accident and had died. Because of the shock at that moment, I didn't know what to do, the only thing that came to my mind was to run through the bushes and disappear, and get away from the bad news, he was my favorite brother. I felt that our hopes and everything he would tell us, were no longer going to be there. He used to tell us to be patient, that he was working very hard, so that our family would be together again.

And so, running through the bushes, I was thinking about all those things that fate had taken away. I felt that we would no longer have hope, I also felt that my heart had gone out of my chest, almost dead from the great pain of losing my brother, who despite everything never forgot his roots and his family. For me that makes him immortal in my heart, and in the middle of the pain and sadness, I told myself you will never die in me, I will always have you present, you will live in my spirit, because the feelings that you awakened in me, showing your marvelous personality for your loved ones, those feelings will be very difficult to erase from my mind.

After that, time went by, and I was growing up, and I felt like doing the same thing he was trying to do with us. But it wasn't that easy, I was just a kid. But the most important thing was that I never forgot about his plans and projects. And in the middle of tears and crying, I was walking through the streets with a 100-degree sun. At that moment I arrived at the cemetery where he was buried, I went to his grave and knelt crying, I asked him to pass on to me, all his virtues and the desire he had to help us, and that he would live in me, so that his wishes would be fulfilled with our family just as he wanted, even though the family was very large. Little by little time passed and I saw the change and how everyone was moving forward in life, I always thought of my family, and I had faith that we would be happy, and have a better life than the one we had; I managed to finish part of my studies, I was able to place a roof over my family's head, and food on the table, without my parents having to kill themselves working, and also, my parents never thought of getting on a plane, it never crossed their minds. I also managed to get one of my younger sisters, 15 years old, to have visions that she was going to have a better future.

And so little by little we were able to reunite the whole family and be with our parents for many years.

Incredible truth! I think that, with so many beautiful things and so many mixed feelings, it is like considering and never forgetting what one as a family can achieve, incredible things, but it was worth it, even though on many occasions I forgot about myself. But it is very important to believe that when you want you can also do it, and that, if every human being did one of the things mentioned in the previous lines, the feelings of each one of us would be more human.

Not only for the family nucleus but also for the rest of humanity, with whom we are surrounded daily.

Observation:
But what if it was me who needed a moment of solidarity, in which they make me feel that I am part of the family, and that when I gave all I could of me, I did it with love. But there came a time when I needed my living siblings, those who could do what a dead person could not do, and realizing that for them I was dead, the only thing I said to myself, that it is incredible that when I was going through something similar in my childhood years, I could count on a

dead brother instead of my living siblings. But the most important thing is to understand that all those around us are our daily mirror and that they don't have the capacity or the will to help their own. So, what will you be able to offer to someone to whom you have no blood ties? Remember, never do anything just for the people around you to notice what you did or didn't do. Because it is better to do something in secret that lasts, than to do something in public openly and let the wind blow away the nice things you may have, because maybe you do not do it for what you feel but because of groundless competitions.

Sexuality

Sexuality is a word that everyone suggests. It seems to be the main theme in us human beings. In the old days we did not see the varieties as we do today. This issue is complicated since it is still restricted, supposedly, until you are of legal age, that is, an adult is not allowed to be with a minor. We all know this, but there are many who do not comply, and they don't do what must be done, without measuring the consequences.

In this world, when you hear any news on the radio or television, you are no longer surprised because these are things, we see every day. When a person commits a crime with a minor, at the end of the day, they end up paying for it.

But when you must live it or witness it daily, for example when it comes to the issue of whether you are gay or straight, it is unusual for us to see it. It is unusual for us to see every day a group of women regardless of age, size, or diseases that person may have.

They only think about pleasure and making the most of their time. Many want to explore and feel that this is their opportunity, especially when they are locked up and sometimes with no way out. They end up becoming lesbians. Many of them, even though they are not lesbians, being female in nature for a moment want to be men. Those who are lesbians really take advantage of those who are straight because that's where they are.

That's the place where no one in their family is watching what they do or don't do. It makes it easy for them to live in a world they never thought they would. In the end, they end up liking it; they think they are making the most of their time.

Sometimes they feel that they died in the world of the street, and they were born in the place where the female sex exists. Many of them They who manage to get out in time to the real world, want to live a normal life with their husbands, but everything becomes a confusion and family storm. The confusion is that now they do not know what they want, if a woman or a man, they can no longer be a family as God left it written.

With all these examples many of us should learn from them. Here I tell you a case of a woman named Lucia. She was about 30 years old when she married another woman, but she was still thinking about her ex-husband. She was very confused and did not know what to do because her wife had a better job than her former husband.

According to the testimonies she got used to certain things that were not her style before. Her husband was still looking for her, he did not know that she was with another woman, when he found out, he went crazy. He could not believe that his wife could betray him with another woman.

What was going through his mind was that he did not satisfy her as a woman and that he was unmanly. His ego collapsed, considering that he was a very "macho" man for that to be happening to him. He couldn't take it anymore, and in the end, Lucia ended up telling him all her truths and the reasons for her decision. She began to reflect on everything that had happened in their relationship.

The man could not hold his anger and he beat her up. Lucia ended up in the hospital with her face and body full of fractures. Fatal consequences that could have been avoided, but that's how we human beings are. We want to be happy no matter what and feel that we are loved by someone. We must make sure that sexuality does not die over time. Many of us want to keep it alive, apart from the feelings, which is what maintains us with the desire to live.

Lonely and sad thought

Loneliness: how hard it is to be alone; they say you are born alone, but if you look at it that way, we are not born alone. Your mother carries you for nine months in her womb and when you are going to be born there are many doctors near your mother waiting for you, that's why you are not really born alone.

How sad that after a while, reality starts to fade away little by little, not knowing what is going on around you and far away. Negative thoughts increase as you don't know anything about your family, sometimes it is impossible to assimilate it, but you can't resign yourself, because you feel that your thinking becomes frozen day after day. You feel dead, and only time heals that wound, what a great sadness that you not only feel, mentally and spiritually bad and between dreams the only thing you can see is your body walking like a zombie and with deep stares.

With frozen eyelashes, with thick tears running down your face. People look at you, they would like to do something for you, but the loneliness and sadness is so great that even if they do a thousand things to make you smile or change your mood, you feel that even the help they offer you saddens you more, you can only wait and pray to God the Almighty, to take out of your soul this deep pain, that I do not wish it to my worst enemy; they say it is better to be alone than in bad company; I agree, but at the same time I think, why does it have to be so? When you are sad you see no sense in life.

All you can do is to talk and comfort yourself because despite everything, you are still standing, and you fight to get up, your tears run like a wellspring, just remembering everything that surrounds you and everything you remember that makes you cry. Sometimes it is very difficult for us because when you remember something, everything makes us cry, even if you don't want to, it is incredible that you can't control yourself. It is so nice to remember the moments we have lived, but at the same time it is so sad, not being able to remember, and trying to avoid the past, present, and future.

We have lived with all these sorrows, but when we think of the most wonderful thing that God has given us in this life, which are our children, to us it is as we never had any of those negative feelings, never experienced them, or ever cried for any of them.

Talent

Talent: We see that some of us are born with a star and others are born shattered. We use that saying because there are people who overnight become famous, and you see them doing soap operas, movies, and TV shows. Most of us human beings are born with a talent, but we don't know how to take advantage of it because of lack of drive, lack of money, or lack of family support. In truth we must follow our instinct to succeed in life, always keep in mind the ambitions and the desire to be someone in the world where we live.

Do not pay attention to the negativities of the people around you, always be yourself, believe in your personality; be consistent, even if you are going through difficult times. We should never stop until we achieve what we want to do in life. That is what will lead you to be a good husband, wife, a good parent, and a good friend. All those feelings together will lead you to be a good human being and follow the path that we all know is a challenge day by day.

As you understand, having talent becomes very attractive for girls, many successes, proposals, and many things that will take you to the top. Try to stay in that position as much as you can.

Sometimes when you have fame you have everything around you, but there can also be a time when you can lose it all. That doesn't mean you're going to run out of money, it means you could be left drained. Since you have everything, sometimes you feel an infinite emptiness inside, it's almost as if you have nothing.

That's why it's good to act as simple as possible, remember who we are and that there are many people out there needing your help. Remember, even if you have what you have, you can help others and you will feel that you want more.

You will try harder, and blessings will fall on you and yours. You will feel happy and eager to continue making other people happy, to the point of never wanting to die. And so, you can turn the happiness and feelings of every human being to an eternity.

Fear

Fear is when they read your diagnosis and your normal temperature suddenly turns into a cyclone, a tornado, and many rains appear, that is, they are frightening you before the time, but there is also fear without warnings, where there are only visions, for fear of some ancestors, as well as fears of diseases, separations of couples, problems with our children; and all these fears together become a nightmare, because they do not allow a happy life.

You don't have peace of mind; in many cases you can't concentrate on your work.

Solution:

If you think about all these fears, you are always going to be a person with mixed feelings; you will never know who you are, and worse, you can get sick of nerves; Our lives are full of fears in different categories, everything has ups and downs, unfortunately we have to live them, we must take into account that when you have to live the moment of fear, as in the case of a lady who was incarcerated for 10 years, and it was time for her release and all her friends and colleagues were very happy, but surprisingly, they noticed that she was nervous and afraid of everything.

Her friends wondered why she was not happy, if she was going to be free in two weeks after 10 years of being locked up, but she was afraid to go to the street, because she had no idea how she was going to face the situation outside, and interact with new people, new jobs, in short, a number of strange things and new technology, which for her is like being born again.

That fear can be overcome and afterwards you will feel that you will be able to float and breathe with security; the only thing you will remember are the visions that you lived in the past, it will only be an experience that can help you in your daily life.

You will feel so much security and inspiration to help your surroundings. There will be no fears, you will be accompanied by people who love you, and all this will give meaning to your life; and everything you do in life will awaken feelings, tenderness, passion, and love for others.

Sadness

When we talk about sadness it can be of any kind. The soul is filled with sadness, it is the deepest feeling because it comes from the heart, it is pure, how helpless you feel knowing that at that moment you are not able to get rid of all the sadness that breaks your heart, because it can lead you to make drastic and confusing decisions.

The only thing that goes through our mind is negativity, you don't even want to exist. Sadness can be temporary as well as permanent, for example, when you are far from your children and you take refuge in something temporary that only causes pain and at the end of the day, time passes, and when you remember what you have suffered you tell yourself: I was such a fool. Suffering is a sign of how happy you can be within a short time. if you have a partner, I think a message of relaxation would help a little.

Intensity:
In my personal life I felt like everything was sad. It practically sounds a little ironic because even though I tried to make things go well, it seemed impossible. For example, in the work area, breaking myself to give my best, and it still wasn't enough, but unfortunately as an employee you would like to receive compliments from your boss, but in turn, instead of making you feel good, considering that you worked all week, they punish by taking away days of work, and that makes you sad, so, why don't they allow you to produce for your family?

If you don't depend on that job, and if the boss tells you, take it or leave it, you have no choice but to look for another job and fulfill your needs. And when you get your second job you also give your best. Then after a few months they stab you in the back and tell you that they no longer need your services. Just because they want to give a job to a relative or someone else. Unfortunately, they don't care about everything that may happen and the sadness that all these things cause you.

Even if it is a bad time and for another human being it is temporary, times come and go, every time they come, you always have in mind that what comes next will be better. But in Rosita's case, she said the opposite, she was going from bad to worse. She felt like a living ghost and there was no happiness in her face.

Her gaze was distant and profound. On some occasions she smiled, although it was superficial, but she always kept the faith and hope that God had something in store for her and that He would put an end to these feelings of sadness, which she sometimes believed to be eternal. You make up your mind to either lock yourself in sadness and/or take refuge in the hope of getting something to live for. Remember, if there is no sadness there is no joy.

Letter to my relatives

Hello, I am Carmencita your daughter, and I am writing this letter to remind you that I am still your daughter, and you are my parents. I always remember you and I never forgot you even though we live in different countries.

Parents will always be parents, and children will always be children. But I would like to tell you a little about myself, since I don't know much about you. I would like to tell you that I am going through very difficult times, and I need your support. As far as I can remember I have never received a kind word, nor have you ever written me a letter of encouragement.

Currently, it is as if I have no father or mother, and I wonder, how does it feel to have children, even if you don't remember them? Anyway, at the end of the day, you are my parents, and I will always love you and of course because of you I have life. In this life we human beings must understand that our parents will always be our parents whether they are near or far away. We must understand that due to life circumstances we as children choose our path. When we choose our path, it is very nice to know that we have parents and that they are alive. In the bottom of our heart, we always have them in our mind as they also have us. As children we must show infinite love no matter the distance; that is what gives meaning to our lives. Especially when our parents are alive, as we know many of us cannot say the same.

This letter is to thank you for all the nice things and all the worries and patience you had when I was little. May God be with you always and may he give you lots of life and blessings. With many kisses and love from your daughter Carmencita.

A light in my eyes

Today begins a challenge for me, because I have 60 days left to see light, light that many would like to see, or hope to get, and that is not so far away. That is why it is very important to make valid decisions in life, those that lead us to make better determinations so that one can have many options to choose from. For example, if you have three options to survive, choose the one you like the most, the one with the least risk.

Something very difficult, because one is never thinking about the worst. It is sad to be punished for crimes not committed, or rather not even given the opportunity to defend yourself. These were many of the cases experienced by women who spent their time crying, suffering from the fact that they were deprived of their freedom. In most cases, there were many years and processes that they had to go through, some deserved, and others not, just to have hope that someday they would see the light in their eyes. Light of hope, of freedom, to breathe air that, even though it might be polluted, simply by the fact of being free, would make you feel and see your dream become a reality.

Knowing that you can touch your children, hug your parents, share with your siblings, friends, and above all have a social life. These are the gifts that one receives by being able to see the light, in our life, and in the beings that love us. The most important light is that of our Lord Jesus Christ who always illuminates the paths to follow, in the difficult life that each one of us must live.

A bloody afternoon

It was a sunny summer afternoon. I had gotten up early to clean my entire house and make some food for myself and my kids. When I finished doing the household chores and started getting ready to go to the gym and take the one-year-old to the day-care, as I was ready to leave the house, I opened the door and what I could see was a cousin of my brother-in-law standing in front of my door, he was my sister's husband's cousin.

I asked him, "What are you doing here, I am on my way out." He answered, "You are not going anywhere." I responded, "What's wrong with you? I don't have time for visits, get out of my way, I must go to the gym." José, my brother-in-law's cousin, didn't listen to me, so he pushed me and closed the door.

The baby started crying, I put him in the crib and tried to get Jose to calm down and leave. Again, he was very shameless, he did not listen to me, nor did he care if the child was crying. So, I asked him, "What do you want?" and he answered, "I have been waiting for a long time, I am in love with you, and you do not pay attention to me, you know that when I want something it has to be mine."

I thought he was joking with me since he is someone I already knew. The furthest thing I could think of was that this man was determined to do what he had in his mind that day. The first thing he did was he looked for a knife in the kitchen and told me, "Take off your clothes if you don't want me to cut your face." I was very scared and told him, "Please don't do something crazy, look the child is crying." He answered: "I don't care!" And shouting, he said it again, "Take off your clothes if you don't want me to cut your face!" I was only 22 years old, he threatened to cut my face. For me, with my face cut, I would never be the same beautiful woman that I had always been. It was a difficult situation; but I had two options, let him cut my face or take off my clothes at that moment. I had no head to make decisions because the child was crying all that time. I felt an overwhelming impotence in that room. I could not cry because my mouth was covered. In a moment of distraction, he tried to push the knife and I was pushing back with my hands.

I was unlucky and it turned out that all five fingers on my hands were cut off until they collapsed. At that moment the world came crashing down on me. The whole house was covered in blood, the wall, the bed, the floor, the child crying and me screaming for help to the neighbors. The murderer had already escaped, taking the knife with him so as not to leave any evidence against him. The neighbors called 911; the firemen, the police and the ambulance arrived.

All the police officers were investigating and looking for evidence to find the person who tried to rape me, but they found no fingerprints. They took me to the hospital and fortunately they were able to save my fingers with 12 stitches in each one. Afterwards I returned home with a broken heart and tried to see my son since my neighbors grabbed him before I went to the hospital.

The boy was still frightened by what he experienced and witnessed on that bloody afternoon. For me the pain was double to know that my son with his innocence witnessed all that cruelty. Just to imagine the helplessness he experienced not being able to do anything for his mother. After that, time passed. I had to receive therapy to overcome the trauma of knowing that I was alive and in a second, I could have been dead. The saddest thing is that a one-year-old child could have witnessed the death of his mother and not be able to be there for him anymore. It's something you don't even want to think about for a moment because even thinking about it hurts.

Interpretation:

We are all exposed to any kind of danger. The most incredible thing is that it doesn't matter if you are at home. Unfortunately, we cannot live in fear. We have the power of the last word, even if it is mentally, to take or choose any road; because if you do not do it, someone else will come and do it for you. Consider that what on this earth you do, on this earth you will pay for it.

Scene:

Two weeks after the incident, the police were looking for the fugitive, but they had no luck; they could never find him. They came to my house to interview me to make the search easier. I told them everything that happened, everything stayed there, and they said they would let me know of any findings. It turned out that two weeks later, they found Mr. José dead with 30 stab wounds in his body. Not even the police could believe that death. To the point that they came back to me because they believed I had something to do with that horrible murder.

They came looking for me at my house a second time, fortunately there was no evidence against me. Then, the investigations continued, and the suspicions were ruled out against me. They continued to investigate elsewhere, although the investigations against me were still open.

Considering that the incident that happened with me and that person was enough to make me want to kill him; but a death like the one Mr. José suffered, I would not wish it even on my worst enemy. How sad, that things like this must happen to a 26-year-old young man just because of his unfulfilled anxiety outbursts. He lost his life early, and if all these situations were to cross our minds, we would avoid many things.

In our mind we know that what we are doing is not right and even if we are angry and we follow our negative intuition, compare it with the future consequences and you will realize that when you compare the before with the after, you will be proud of the positive decisions you made at that time.

You will see the gains you are going to have, which will help you forget the difficult bad moment that was not easy to process. We must practice as if you were doing yoga. This does not mean that you are going to expose yourself to any kind of danger, what I mean is that you follow your natural instincts so that you can enjoy the life that God and your mother want, and how much you must do. May your death not have to be at an early age; when it could be after you have fulfilled all your purposes for you and your family.

These are real life events, and we take the time and moment to explain how difficult it is when you have no control and get carried away by anger. It's a matter of making choices; either you destroy yourself or you rise. When you rise, we call it being born and living until natural death. By that time, you would have fulfilled the purposes of the destiny God chose for you.

Permanent revenge

Permanent revenge sounds a bit strong; it means that you will always suffer and never rest, but there are many types of revenge, from couples, death, boyfriends, friends, or inheritance. All of these come from emotionally affected people, and they seek to satisfy themselves so that their enemies feel the same pain as they do. Revenge is fearful because it can end in death and in many cases even worse, many prefer to die than to be in a coma, since this way they do not suffer and when the person is vengeful, he does not think about the consequences.

Scene.

A lady named Dulce, who by coincidence met a man and apparently, they both had many things in common. Dulce only saw him as a friend and tried to avoid any kind of love contact because she had been living alone for some time and felt comfortable that way. But this man, would every day behave in a convincing way and so the years went by and finally she decided to give him a chance. They started a nice romantic relationship to see if it would work. And it really did work.

They both did their part, they made a lot of sacrifices, however, they had a past that still haunted them, and that hurt the relationship to some extent. But they kept working together anyway, not because it was love at first sight, but because she had suffered a lot and was tired. So, she tried to get along with him. Calcio gave 100% with this relationship. But for Dulce came a difficult moment where he had to go to jail for a while. Calcio had been left in charge of everything. Since there were a lot of things at stake, and he was the only person she could trust at that time. He told her not to worry about anything because everything was going to be fine, since when they lived together, he convinced her that she could trust him blindly, and as time went by, things started to go wrong. It wasn't even half of what she lived with him before. The man became an alcoholic. He went out every night and at all hours and didn't keep the things he promised her. He went from bad to worse.

He only received criticism from the family. Later, everything came to light, he was seeing other women without caring that Dulce could find out. For Dulce it was double suffering, because she could not do anything, no matter how much she wanted to do something, it was almost impossible and even worse when she found out that when she got to jail, they did all the medical exams and found out she was pregnant, it was shocking for her because she was making sure not to get pregnant. It was not pleasant at all. She decided to have the baby thinking that it would make him change, but it didn't. Even though he was asking God to have a child, especially with Dulce, saying he loved her, a lot of things were going through Dulce's mind.

She couldn't believe that after making such a difficult decision, to have someone by her side, things would end up that way. What was going through her mind was not pleasant at all, little by little she was planning how she was going to take revenge on that person. That was when it was time for him to leave. She arrived at the house and began to act normal so that he would not discover her plans for revenge and make him believe that she had forgotten everything. She was only going to do one or two things; she was going to leave him scarred forever. At that time, he still hadn't seen his daughter.

Dulce scene:

She told him that she wanted to make love to him aggressively, and that she had to tie his hands and feet to make love to him. He agreed, since every man likes to live out his fantasies. Everything was ready for the action, and he allowed for himself to be tied up and he was very happy and could not imagine anything in his mind and said, I am the happiest man in the world. I am back with my wife, and she gave me a beautiful daughter.

Action:

She had everything written down on a piece of paper and every day she would read the notes that smacked with the smell of revenge. Then she said, "You think you're going to have a good time, don't you?" Calcio started to change his face because the attitude Dulce had was not one of happiness. She began to mention each of the written things and each one had a punishment.

She told him, "For cheating on me, I'm going to cut off your genitals, so that you will cry and suffer and feel like dying for not keeping your promises... I will pierce your stomach with metal pincers for not thanking me for giving you a daughter... I will burn your face." Then Dulce told him, "Take a little rest... the punishments don't end there." She began to hit him in the back, he couldn't take it anymore. He screamed and screamed, "Please don't kill me!" But that was not Dulce's intention.

Her intention was to punish him so that he would never forget all his nastiness and that he would never want to do it again. But things didn't stop there. Dulce covered him with a black mantle, and she only left his eyes out. The shock of seeing his daughter, was so great and the poor reaction he could have at that moment, was that he would rather be dead than to see his daughter. For him, not being able to hold his daughter was stronger than what Dulce had already done to him. Dulce already calls it permanent revenge, since he would never forget these moments of fantasy, which he thought he was going to live with his wife. Dulce took him out of the place, while he was still tied up, and brought him to an apartment that did not belong to anyone, abandoning him to his fate.

Interpretation:

Even if it is a permanent revenge, there is no death that could compensate what he lived in that time, although it was not a revenge of death, the satisfaction was that he was not going to do it again. For Dulce that was enough. That's the way we humans are, we hurt other people's feelings to the point that they feel awful. I also want to emphasize that I do not recommend any of you to practice this with anyone, because, just as Dulce thought it was a permanent revenge on him, it was also a permanent revenge on her, since every time she would see her daughter, she would be reminded of the victim every day. In her mind, Dulce believed it was more than a revenge, because she knew that he would never be happy in his entire life.

Definition:

Dulce always says that when we decide to take revenge against any other person, thinking that it will make us happier the problem will end. Unfortunately, that is not the case, if you don't think about it before doing it, the problem will become even stronger and you will live in torment throughout your life, and so on. It only takes seconds for your feelings to die or live. It depends on you, taking one moment, a yes or a no. This story was based on real facts with the purpose of becoming aware of the consequences.

Travel

When we talk about travel, we always think of a person over 60 years old. And when we refer to them, sometimes we don't pay much attention to them as if they were nobody and what they have to say does not matter. And we do not consider that older people may be more important than us, young people; first because they are our parents, our grandparents, great-grandparents, and we all learn from them.

It is important to realize and think that every older person was one of us in the past. Since we, young people are going to become one of those elderly persons someday. We know this, but we do not carefully contemplate the beauty of aging. The beauty of it all is that we become like children again, and we are cared for as if we were babies.

They bathe us, put food in our mouths, paint our nails, etc. We must recognize that no matter how old or young we are, just because we are young does not mean that we should diminish an older person. In many cases there are many older people who have more energy than a young person; the reason, I don't know.

We must also remember that when we have any kind of illness, it is not because we are old, it means that, even if you are young, you can get sick. It is important to have admiration not only for an adult, but for each of our brothers and sisters, and all the people around us. Because one never knows the necessities that someone may have, if we are not old it means that we were never young. In a way, what gets wrinkles is the skin, not the heart or your way of thinking.

And remember that when you find an old man or woman on your way, look at them as a mirror, until you realize that it is you; help them if they need it, and you will discover a huge satisfaction as you have never felt before. When you grow older you will realize when someone does it with you, and you will remember that moment when you were able to help someone. You will know that everything in your life is valuable, even the smallest things that you've forgot, but at the same time all those memories will come to your mind.

About the writer

This biography is based on real facts, for all of us, in general we must interpret that the lie that was already mentioned, no matter how small it maybe it will never take us to a positive place to become a better person and to make ourselves known as we really are. For in that manner, we will be respected, and welcomed wherever we may be; and remember that our personality and actions are what will always matter in life, to become candidates and deservers of the successes that many of us earn day by day.

Reminder:
Every morning we should say who we are and what we want, especially mentioning what we desire, our eternal happiness, as an example to others.

SCAN THE CODES

Los Bori y Los Domi - Ñoñi la Distinguida

Papi no me mientas - Ñoñi La

Tus Mahones - Ñoñi La Distinguida

Disclosure:
If you want to learn more about the author,
you can access this code that contains the
reality show, produced, and performed by
the author, empowering women.
One Woman Ms. Universe.
When scanning, there is a cost.

This **QR** belongs to the foundation of the
author of the book.
Sloth King Foundation.
Seeking help to give help.

SOFT COVER:

9798399283296

Made in the USA
Middletown, DE
21 August 2023

36799036R00117